The Legends of
WOLVERHAMPTON WANDERERS

The Legends of WOLVERHAMPTON WANDERERS

by Tony Matthews

breedon books
PUBLISHING

First published in Great Britain in 2006 by
The Breedon Books Publishing Company
Limited
Breedon House, 3 The Parker Centre,
Derby, DE21 4SZ.

ISBN 1 85983 518 X

Printed and bound by BIDDLES LTD,
King's Lynn, Norfolk.

Contents

Introduction and Acknowledgements

To choose 100 legends from any one club that has been in existence for more than 125 years is no easy task. And, therefore, I am expecting a few supporters to ask the question, why wasn't his or her favourite player included?

If I had been allowed to feature 200 legends, I don't think there would be any problems, no queries as to who should and shouldn't be included, but I went for men who I believe gave Wolverhampton Wanderers football club excellent service over a number of years.

I would like to thank Graham Hughes, the Wolves historian and a great friend of mine, club photographer Peter Harrington of Ivanhoe Photography for copying the photographs from Wolverhampton Wanderers Archives, Steve Caron and Susan Last at Breedon Books and also love and thanks to my darling wife Margaret for her terrific support and, indeed, patience!

And last but my no means last, I say thank you to the 100 legends themselves....if it hadn't been for them this book would have been rather nondescript.

Read and enjoy.

Tony Matthews, June 2006

JACK ADDENBROOKE

Date of birth: 6 June 1865, Wolverhampton
Died: 7 September 1922, Wolverhampton

Wolves record:
Secretary-manager: August 1885 to June 1922

Jack Addenbrooke attended and played for St Luke's School, Blakenhall, for five years from 1873–78. In fact, he was made secretary of the football team in the playground at the age of 10. After attending Saltley College, Birmingham, for two years (1879–81), he was employed as a teacher at Bushbury School, Wolverhampton, and in the summer of 1883 he was persuaded to join Wolves as a reserve forward.

Playing regularly for the second team, Addenbrooke's affection for the club grew enormously, so much so that in August 1885 he was appointed as the first paid secretary-manager of Wolverhampton Wanderers FC while still registered as a player, although he decided to retire from that side of the game 12 months later. He was to remain in office as secretary-manager for 37 years – until 1922 – the longest reign by a manager in Wolves' history.

During his wonderful association with the club, Addenbrooke, a tall, upright gentleman with smart moustache who always wore a hat out of doors, saw Wolves establish themselves in the Football League, twice win the FA Cup in 1893 and 1908, claim the runners'-up prize in the same competition three times, in 1889, 1896 and 1921, triumph in several local competitions, including winning the Birmingham, Lord Mayor of Birmingham Charity and Staffordshire Cups and, above all, become one of the top clubs in English football.

In 1909 the Football League celebrated 21 years of existence, and to mark the occasion Addenbrooke and his close friend George Ramsey, the Aston Villa secretary, were both presented with long-service medals by the League. He later became a director and then president of the Staffordshire FA, serving on the committee for 28 years.

Besides being an exceptional office worker (he knew everything there was to know about being the secretary of a company), Addenbrooke also ran a tobacconist's shop in Wolverhampton. And he could certainly spot a good footballer when he saw one. Among those he signed for Wolves (with the assistance of others, including scouts and ex-professionals) were goalkeepers Tom Baddeley, Noel George, Tommy Lunn, Teddy Peers, William Crispin Rose and Billy Tennant; defenders Harry Allen, Dickie Baugh, Alf Bishop, Arthur Fletcher, George Garratly, Val Gregory, Jack Jones, George Kinsey, Billy Malpass, Charlie Mason and George Swift; the Reverend Kenneth Hunt and George Fleming; the versatile Billy Woodridge; wingers Sammy Brooks, Billy Harrison, Jack Miller and Jack Pedley; and forwards Billy Beats, George Edmonds, Willie Halligan, George Hedley, Ted Pheasant, Harry Wood and David Wykes. Several of these players became internationals as well as giving Wolves wonderful service.

Addenbrooke held the Molineux fort manfully during World War One and was certainly responsible for arranging and overseeing major developments at the ground. When League football recommenced in 1919, he was at the heart of everything – sorting out players' contracts, making a few extra signings and generally running the club single-handed. Unfortunately, all this hard work took its toll. Having complained of headaches and breathing difficulties for several weeks, he was taken ill in June 1922, and on the 25th of that month he was declared unfit for work by the club doctor, Mr Richard Wolverson. He was allowed six months leave, but sadly he never left hospital. His health deteriorated, and on 7 September 1922 he passed away, aged 57.

Mr Albert Hoskins took over his duties as club secretary, with George Jobey assuming the role of manager-coach to the team.

HARRY ALLEN

Date of birth: 19 January 1866, Walsall
Died: 23 February 1895, Walsall

Wolves record:
Appearances: League 123, FA Cup 30
Goals: League 8, FA Cup 5
Debut: FA Cup, 30 October 1886 v Matlock (h) won 6–0

Also played for: Walsall Town Swifts, England (5 caps)

Although a little imprudent at times, Harry Allen was a splendid centre-half and captain of Wolves. He was quite unflagging, especially good in the air, strong in the tackle and a fine passer of the ball, who always tried to find a teammate when clearing his lines rather than simply hoofing it into the air in hope rather than judgement, that is, of course, unless he was forced to resort to desperate measures to avert possible danger.

After making his mark with Walsall Town Swifts, Allen joined Wolves at the start of the 1886–87 season at the age of 20 and scored on his senior debut for the club in a 6–0 FA Cup win over Matlock Town, two months after his arrival. He scored again in his second Cup appearance when Crosswell's Brewery were thrashed 14–0 – this being Wolves' record victory in major competitive football.

Virtually an ever present in his first two seasons, during which time he won three of his five England caps, playing against Wales and twice against Scotland during February and March 1888, Allen lined up for Wolves in their first Football League game against Aston Villa at Dudley Road on 8 September 1888. He had an excellent match and, in fact, was one of only two players to appear in all 28 competitive League and Cup matches that season, the other being right-back Dickie Baugh. It was, however, bitterly disappointing for Allen and his colleagues when Wolves lost to double-winners Preston North End 3–0 in the FA Cup Final at the Oval. A fortnight later he returned to the Surrey cricket ground to play for England against Scotland, and once again he was on the losing side, this time by 3–2.

Absent from just one League game in 1889–90, the season which also saw him gain his final cap versus Scotland, Allen continued to give his all for Wolves. He was outstanding week after week, and with wing-halves Arthur Fletcher and Arthur Lowder also performing excellently, Wolves finished fourth in the League table, eight points behind the champions Preston. The same position was claimed the following season when Jack Brodie occasionally figured alongside Allen at left-half, Wolves missing out on the title by three points on this occasion.

Not surprisingly, the team was built around Allen, and in 1891–92 future England international George Kinsey came into the half-back line. Wolves, though, slipped down two places in the League table despite some solid displays by Allen and his co-defenders.

With more of a settled line up in 1892–93, Wolves had a moderate League campaign, but in the FA Cup they played superbly well, Allen included, and went all the way to the Final, where they met Everton at Fallowfield, Manchester. Sleeves rolled up, with cropped hair and trimmed moustache, he drove his players on with great enthusiasm, as always, and after 60 minutes he fired home the winning goal to send the Wolves supporters in the 45,000 crowd into raptures. It was not a pretty goal but it was a very valuable one, gained by sheer pluck and endeavour from the player who was named Man of the Match (not for the first time either).

Allen made only 12 further League appearances for Wolves after that Cup success. Illness coupled with a back injury forced him to retire in October 1894, and he took over a pub in Wolverhampton. Sadly, in February 1895, he died suddenly, aged 29.

TOM BADDELEY

Date of birth: 2 November 1874, Bycars, Burslem, Stoke-on-Trent
Died: 24 September 1946, Hartshill, Stoke-on-Trent

Wolves record:
Appearances: League 296, FA Cup 19
Goals: 0
Debut: League, 1 September 1897 v Preston North End (h) won 3–0

Also played for: Burslem Swifts, Burslem Port Vale, Bradford Park Avenue, Stoke and Whitfield Colliery, England (5 caps)

An excellent goalkeeper, brave and consistent with outstanding agility and capable of dealing with any type of shot, Tom Baddeley spent 18 years in the game, 11 of them with Wolves, and was the first player to appear in 300 senior matches for the club.

A shade on the small side for a player in his position, Baddeley was only 5ft 9in tall but was never afraid to go in where it hurt, often diving at the feet of opponents as well as contesting for high balls with the rugged, powerful centre-forwards of his era. He could also throw the ball downfield up to 50 yards and regularly turned defence into attack with one almighty swing of his right arm.

Baddeley was 19 when he made his senior debut for Burslem Port Vale – the team he had supported as a lad – and was an ever present in their ranks for two seasons (1894–95 and 1895–96) before joining Wolves for £50 in October 1896, when he was signed as cover for Billy Tennant. He spent the remainder of that season in the second team before finally making the first of 315 senior appearances for Wolves at the start of the 1897–98 campaign following Tennant's transfer to Walsall. He performed exceedingly well as Wolves finished third in the League table, missing only one game and conceding 41 goals in 30 Division One matches.

Baddeley continued to impress between the posts and, injuries apart, remained first choice at Molineux until March 1907 when he was replaced by Tommy Lunn, who had been with the club for three years. At the peak of his form, during the 1902–03 and 1903–04 seasons, he gained England recognition. He won the first of five caps against Ireland on his own patch (Molineux) in February 1903, starring in a 4–0 win. Others followed against Scotland at Sheffield four weeks later, versus Wales at Wrexham, against Ireland in Belfast and versus Scotland at Celtic Park during March and April 1904. In fact, 40,000 fans saw him produce five brilliant saves in his last international, which England won 1–0.

Baddeley was lucky not to suffer too many injuries during his career. He was out of action only half a dozen times, mainly due to a back problem, although he did dislocate his finger and damage his shoulder twice.

Making his last appearance for Wolves against Burton United (away) in March 1907 (lost 4–1), at the end of that season Baddeley left Molineux to become a founder member of Bradford Park Avenue. He played in the Yorkshire club's first-ever League game against Hull City in September 1908 but surprisingly failed to hold down a regular place in the side. He switched his allegiance to Stoke in March 1910, and after a handful of games for the Potters he wound down his career in non-League football with Whitfield Colliery, eventually retiring in May 1911 at the age of 36.

MIKE BAILEY

Date of birth:	27 February 1942, Wisbech, Cambridgeshire
Wolves record:	
Appearances:	League 360+1, FA Cup 18+2, League Cup 29, Europe 9+1, Others 16
Goals:	League 19, FA Cup 2, League Cup 0, Europe 1, Others 2
Debut:	League, 12 March 1966 v Southampton (h) drew 1–1
Also played for:	Charlton Athletic, Minnesota Kicks (NASL), Hereford United (player-manager), Bexley Heath (player-manager), England (5 Under-23 & 2 full caps)
Managed:	Charlton Athletic, Brighton and Hove Albion, Fisher Athletic, Leatherhead

Mike Bailey suffered two massive injury scares during his time with Charlton Athletic. In September 1962 – two years after making his League debut – he severely damaged his right shoulder in a game against Scunthorpe United. Thankfully he made a full recovery, but then, in February 1965, he suffered a double fracture of his left leg playing against Middlesbrough in an FA Cup fourth-round replay. This knocked him back considerably, and he was out of action for eight months, during which time he underwent a great deal of strenuous and tedious work in the gym. Once again Bailey bounced back, regained full fitness, his confidence and self-belief and, indeed, his form and developed into one of the finest half-backs in the country, as well as being an inspirational captain at both Charlton and Wolves.

Bailey scored 22 goals in 169 first-class matches for Charlton, whom he served from 1957 as an amateur and from 1959 as a professional. He won all his England honours during his time at The Valley – his two senior caps coming against the USA in May 1964 (when he starred in a 10–0 win) and versus Wales six months later (won 2–1). He also represented the Football League on three occasions, having played for Norfolk County and Kent youth teams earlier in his career.

Bailey moved to Molineux in February 1966, signed by manager Ronnie Allen for a bargain fee of just £35,000, and the following season he was outstanding as Wolves regained their top-flight status by finishing runners-up to Coventry City in Division Two. He missed only one League game that season when he proved to be the vital cog in a wonderful midfield engine that also comprised colleagues Ernie Hunt, Davey Burnside and Peter Knowles, and he was voted Midlands Footballer of the Year.

Quickly adapting to life in the top Division, Bailey was now the team's driving force as he produced some outstanding performances, helping Wolves finish fourth in the table in 1971 and win the Texaco Cup Final. The following season he led the team to the UEFA Cup Final where they lost on aggregate to Tottenham Hotspur, and two years after that he was as proud as punch when he walked up the 39 steps to Wembley's royal box to collect the League Cup after Wolves had beaten Manchester City 2–1 in the Final.

Unfortunately Wolves started to struggle in the League in the mid 1970s, claiming 12th place two seasons running before being relegated in 1976 after one of the worst campaigns since World War Two when they lost over half of their 42 games. At this juncture, Bailey was starting to feel the pinch. Nevertheless, after a well-deserved testimonial match against West Bromwich Albion, he battled on gamely and made another 10 appearances in 1976–77 as Wolves won the Second Division Championship at the first attempt. This turned out to be his last season at Molineux, and with Steve Daley, Kenny Hibbitt and Willie Carr manning midfield efficiently he left Molineux for life in America, joining Minnesota Kicks for £15,000 as player and assistant-coach.

In June 1978 he returned to the UK with Hereford United as player-manager and later served his former club Charlton as a scout and manager, steering the Addicks to promotion in 1981. He also had a decent spell in charge of Brighton & Hove Albion and worked a minor miracle by keeping Fisher Athletic in the GM Vauxhall Conference in 1990.

JOHN BARNWELL

Date of birth: 24 December 1938, High Heaton, Newcastle-upon-Tyne

Wolves record:
Manager: November 1978 to January 1982

Played for: Bishop Auckland, Arsenal, Nottingham Forest, Sheffield United.
Also managed: Peterborough United, AEK Athens (Greece), Notts County, Walsall, England (1 Under-23 cap)

As a player, John Barnwell was a powerful, workmanlike and very effective inside-forward who started his career with the amateur club Bishop Auckland. He moved to Highbury in 1955 and went on to score 24 goals in 155 first-class matches for Arsenal, whom he served for eight years until 1964 when he transferred to Nottingham Forest for £30,000. He added a further 25 goals to his tally in 201 games during his six years at the City Ground before having a spell with Sheffield United, where he scored two goals in 13 matches.

An England Youth international who went on to gain one Under-23 cap as well as representing the RASC during his national service, Barnwell retired as a player in 1971, at which point he took over as coach at Hereford United, remaining at Edgar Street for just 13 weeks. His next position (as coach) took him to Peterborough United, who appointed him as manager in May 1977, a position he held until November 1978 when he walked out just six months before missing promotion to the Second Division.

After only a short break from football, during which time he applied for the vacant manager's job at Sunderland, missing out to former Wolves player Ken Knighton, Barnwell was successful when he put his name forward for the position as manager at Molineux, taking over the hot seat in November 1978, and he remained in office until January 1982, when he was sacked.

Barnwell quickly turned things round on the pitch and at the end of that season came mighty close to taking Wolves to the FA Cup Final, losing in the semi-final to his former club Arsenal 2–0 at Villa Park. However, shortly afterwards he almost lost his life in a road traffic accident, which saw him hospitalised with a fractured skull. Richie Barker took over as caretaker boss, with player-coach Brian Garvey assisting too. Thankfully he recovered in time for the start of the new season, and virtually straightaway he bolstered up his defence by signing the Liverpool and England star Emlyn Hughes for a bargain fee of just £90,000. Soon afterwards he set the world talking when he smashed the British transfer record by selling midfielder Steve Daley to Manchester City for £1,437,500 (5 September), and then, 72 hours later, he paid out £1,150,000 for the Aston Villa striker Andy Gray. Winger David Thomas also arrived from QPR and all of a sudden there was a buzz of excitement within the club.

The team's League performances, however, were rather inconsistent on the pitch, and Barnwell wasn't too happy. Yet in the League Cup it was all so different, as slowly but surely Wolves edged their way to the Final. They got there, and on 15 March 1980 he proudly led his players out at Wembley to take on his former club Nottingham Forest, managed by Brian Clough. A tight game ended in triumph for Wolves, Andy Gray's tap-in goal deciding the contest to book Wolves a place in the UEFA Cup.

Barnwell was very optimistic about the 1980–81 season, and he actually made enquiries about the availability of the French international Michel Platini and Poland's Ziggy Boniek but had to settle for the Uruguayan Rafael Villazan instead. However, Wolves did not have a happy season. They finished 18th in the First Division, went out of the League and UEFA Cup competitions in the opening round and lost in the FA Cup semi-final to Tottenham Hotspur in a replay. Again he went out and signed new players, but, after starting 1981–82 with a 1–0 home win over Liverpool, suddenly everything started to go wrong again, and after a series of defeats Wolves found themselves at the wrong end of the table – as a result he lost his job, having his contract terminated in January 1982.

Obviously disappointed, Barnwell subsequently had a spell in Saudi Arabia before becoming coach of AEK Athens, only to be banned from working in Greece in January 1984. Three years later he took over as manager of Notts County and held a similar position with Walsall (1989–90) before becoming a consultant at Northampton Town (1992–93). He was appointed chief executive of the Football League Managers' Association in July 1997 and has also been involved with Grantham Town.

DICKIE BAUGH (senior)

Date of birth:	14 February 1864, Wolverhampton
Died:	14 August 1929, Wolverhampton

Wolves record:

Appearances:	League 185, FA Cup 42
Goals:	League 1, FA Cup 0
Debut:	FA Cup first round, 30 March 1886 v Matlock (h) won 6–0.
Also played for:	Rose Villa, Wolverhampton Rangers, Stafford Road FC, Walsall, England (1 cap)

Dickie Baugh was a redoubtable defender, zealous, clean-kicking and with a tremendous appetite for hard work. A well-built player, he was also quick in recovery and a powerful header of the ball. Yet despite his aggressiveness, he was never sent off and rarely cautioned by the referee a rare achievement among players of today's game.

A former pupil at St Luke's School in Blakenhall, Baugh was 22 years of age when he joined Wolves as a professional in March 1886 from the well-established local railway club Stafford Road. While playing with them, he gained his first England cap versus Ireland in March 1886. He immediately established himself in the first team, partnering Charlie Mason at full-back and, in fact, both players were ever present in the first season of League football in 1888–89, and they also played in the 3–0 FA Cup Final defeat by Preston North End at The Oval.

The following year, in March 1890, both Baugh and Mason were named as England's full-backs for the home international against Ireland in Belfast. It was his second cap and Mason's third – and they helped their country to an emphatic 9–1 win.

Two more FA Cup Final appearances came Baugh's way as a Wolves player. In 1893 he was outstanding in a hard-fought 1–0 win over Everton at Fallowfield, Manchester, and three years later he collected a second runners'-up medal when Sheffield Wednesday won a tight game 2–1 at Crystal Palace.

After 10 years' service and more than 220 senior appearances for Wolves, all at right-back, plus one goal scored in a 3–3 League draw with Liverpool at Anfield in December 1894, Baugh was perhaps surprisingly transferred to neighbouring Walsall for a small fee in the summer of 1896. He remained with the Saddlers for only one season before announcing his retirement due to a knee injury, which had been troubling him for quite some time.

Only six players have appeared in more FA Cup games for Wolves than Baugh, who, without doubt, was a genuinely fine footballer and a loyal and dedicated club man, who continued to attend matches at Molineux right up until his death. In fact, he was mainly responsible for his son, Richard Baugh junior, joining Wolves in 1918. He later assisted Cardiff City (briefly), West Bromwich Albion, Exeter City and Kidderminster Harriers.

JACK BAYNTON

Date of birth:	20 March 1859, Rushtock Wood, Worcestershire
Died:	17 May 1939, Alfreton, Derbyshire

Wolves record:

Appearances:	League 18, FA Cup 10
Goals:	0
Debut:	FA Cup, 27 October 1883 v Long Eaton Rangers (h) won 4–1
Also played for:	Kidderminster Olympic

Although he made only 28 appearances in competitive football, Jack Baynton (christened John) was one of the most inspirational and respected players in Wolves' early years. A pupil-teacher at St Luke's School, Blakenhall, for whom he played as a centre-half, he helped form Wolverhampton Wanderers football club in 1877 with his best friend John Brodie.

Baynton was only 12 months old when, along with his family, he moved from Rushtock Wood to Lodge Farm on Goldthorn Hill, Wolverhampton, where he was to remain for the next 60 years, during which time he saw the club emerge as one of the biggest and, at times, strongest in the country. On several occasions he captained the team while also acting as the club's treasurer and secretary of St Luke's School. Indeed, he was skipper when Wolves won their first ever trophy – the Wrekin Cup in 1884.

A versatile footballer who occupied eight different positions during his short career, Baynton was a registered player with Wolves from the outset in September 1877 until April 1889, when he signed for Kidderminster Olympic, with whom he stayed for one season. His last senior outing for Wolves came in March 1889, in the FA Cup Final against double-chasing Preston North End. Unfortunately Wolves were no match for the Invincibles from Deepdale and were soundly beaten 3–0 at The Oval.

Baynton was in goal in that Final, but earlier he had performed admirably at right-back, in all three half-back positions, at inside-right, centre-forward and inside-left. It is on record that in one local Cup game he scored a goal from almost 100 yards, fly-kicking the ball downfield, one bounce, over his opposite number's head and over the line.

Not a very tall or, indeed, well-built footballer – he stood at 5ft 9in in his bare feet and weighed 11st – Baynton declared, after retiring early in 1890, that he always preferred to keep goal and, in fact, he stood between the posts for Wolves' first-ever League game against Aston Villa at Dudley Road in September 1888 when he produced some excellent saves (many with his feet) in a 1–1 draw. Five years earlier he also starred in Wolves' first FA Cup tie against Long Eaton Rangers, but this time he was a centre-half.

In the 1888–89 season Baynton appeared in the first 18 of Wolves' 22 League games. He also starred in all six FA Cup ties, having a superb game in the third round when The Wednesday were defeated 3–0 and in the semi-final replay when the 1886 winners Blackburn Rovers were beaten 3–1. When he decided to leave Wolves at the age of 30 – due to school commitments – Jack was replaced in goal by Billy Crispin Rose, who had deputised for him in the last four League matches. Then, as Kidderminster Olympic's goalkeeper, he once sat in a chair in his goalmouth, happily smoking a pipe, watching his colleagues thump Hereford Thistle 25–0 in a Birmingham Cup tie.

Jack remained in close contact with Wolves over the next 10 years, but once he had settled into his new job – as an English and Maths teacher at All Saints School, Hockley, Birmingham – he spent most of his weekends refereeing, following in the footsteps of his buddy Jack Brodie. He also enjoyed a game of cricket and was a very capable swimmer. He was 80 years of age when he died in Derbyshire in 1939 – a month after Wolves had lost to Portsmouth in the FA Cup Final.

BILLY BEATS

Date of birth:	13 November 1871, Wolstanton, Stoke-on-Trent
Died:	6 April 1939, Reading

Wolves record:

Appearances:	League 199, FA Cup 19
Goals:	League 67, FA Cup 6
Debut:	League, 2 September 1895 v Burnley (h) won 5–1
Also played for:	Porthill Victoria, Port Vale Rovers, Burslem Port Vale (two spells), Bristol Rovers, Reading, England (2 caps)

An out-and-out centre-forward, keen and aggressive with a powerful right-foot shot, Billy Beats joined Wolves in June 1895 for £80 plus a guarantee of a further £50 from of an arranged benefit match, after scoring 32 goals in 107 first-team games for Burslem Port Vale, whom he served for four years, his hat-trick helping them beat Wolves 4–1 in the Final of the Staffordshire Cup in March 1894.

Beats loved to run at defenders, but he was also a clever footballer in his own right, often deceiving his opponents with smart footwork or by dropping his shoulder and turning completely round with or without the ball. A lot of his goals were scored with deliberate or well-directed shots, several from inside the penalty area, although at times he would choose to unleash a stinging drive from fully 20–25 yards.

Beats spent eight seasons at Molineux, during which time he accumulated an exceptionally fine record. He also represented England against Wales in March 1901 (won 6–0) and Scotland in May 1902 (drew 2–2), and he also played in that ill-fated international match against Scotland at Ibrox Park, Glasgow, in April 1902 when 25 spectators were killed and over 500 injured, some of them seriously, after wooden terracing collapsed behind one of the goals. This game, which ended level at 1–1, was subsequently declared unofficial and deleted from the records.

A regular in the Wolves side from the day he scored on his senior debut against Burnley on the opening day of the 1895–96 season until shortly after the start of the 1902–03 campaign, Beats finished up as leading marksman for the club twice, and in terms of goals scored his best season was his first when he netted 14 in the League and Cup, collecting an FA Cup runners'-up medal after defeat by Sheffield Wednesday in the Final. Towards the end of his Molineux career he began to lose his form, although an ankle injury didn't help his cause. He made 18 appearances in his last season with the club when he had to battle for his place in the front line with Jack Smith, who had arrived from Stafford Road in July 1902.

Leaving reluctantly in the summer of 1903, Beats joined Bristol Rovers and two years later returned to Burslem Port Vale. However, in May 1907, after adding a further 12 goals to his tally with the Valiants, he was sold to Reading when the club found themselves in financial difficulty and were officially wound up, losing their League status as a result.

In the summer of 1911 Beats was appointed trainer of his former club Bristol Rovers, and a year or so later he took up a similar position at Reading. He retired from the game in May 1917 and became a publican, taking over the Truro Inn in Castle Street, Reading.

Manager Jack Addenbrooke persuaded Billy to join Wolves when he was working on a chapel roof... refusing to let him come down until he promised his signature.

GOOD YEAR

GARY BELLAMY

Date of birth:	4 July 1962, Worksop, Notts.
Wolves record:	
Appearances:	League 133+3, FA Cup 3, League Cup 9, Others 16
Goals:	League 9, FA Cup 0, League Cup 0, Others 0
Debut:	League, 12 September 1987 v Crewe Alexandra (h) drew 2–2
Also played for:	Chesterfield, Cardiff City, Leyton Orient, Chelmsford City
Managed:	Dover Athletic

Signed in September 1987 by manager Graham Turner for £17,000 from Chesterfield, for whom he had appeared in more than 200 competitive games, defender Gary Bellamy made his debut for Wolves only 48 hours after joining the club, but thereafter he had to work hard to gain a regular place in the side due to the form of fellow defender Steve Stoutt.

Partnering Andy Thompson, Bellamy actually shared the right-back duties with Stoutt during that season, helping Wolves win the Fourth Division Championship (just like he had done with his former club Chesterfield in 1985) and also lift the Sherpa Van Trophy at Wembley, beating Burnley 2–0 in the Final in front of 80,841 supporters.

Capable of playing in the centre-half position as well (and as the anchor-man in midfield if required), Bellamy certainly bolstered up a previously leaky Wolves defence, and over the next four years he produced some terrific performances as the Molineux side charged through the Third Division and into the Second in rapid time. His positive, tireless displays down the right flank enabled Wolves to attack much more than in the past, and in some cases he was classed as an extra forward, a winger in fact, whose crosses were usually delivered into the danger-zone to perfection for the lethal and prolific striker Steve Bull and his partner up front Andy Mutch.

Bellamy played in 24 League games in his first season at Molineux, starred in 43 in his second, had 39 outings in his third and appeared in 26 in his fourth, skippering the side from time to time before losing his place to new signing Kevin Ashley.

Remaining at the club as an important and certainly valuable reserve, Bellamy had a successful loan spell with Cardiff City between March and May 1992, during which time he gained a Welsh Cup-winners' medal. And then, after a long discussion with his manager, he chose pastures new by moving south to Leyton Orient for a fee of £30,000 soon after the start of the 1992–93 season. He added a further 150 games to his tally with the London club before quitting top-class football in May 1996, at which time he was appointed player-coach and commercial manager of non-League side Chelmsford City, later taking charge of the Nationwide Conference side Dover Athletic.

RT WOLVES NEW LO

GEORGE BERRY

Date of birth: 19 November 1957, Rostrop, West Germany

Wolves record:
Appearances: League 124, FA Cup 21, League Cup 14, Europe 1
Goals: League 4, FA Cup 2, League Cup 0, Europe 0
Debut: League, 7 May 1977 v Chelsea (h) drew 1–1.

Also played for: Stoke City, Doncaster Rovers, Peterborough United, Preston North End, Aldershot, Stafford Rangers, Wales (5 caps)

George Berry, loose-limbed with a deceptively casual style, was nonetheless a strong-tackling, determined and wholehearted central defender who became a firm favourite with the fans at Molineux.

Born in Germany to a Welsh mother and a Jamaican father, Berry came over to England as a youngster and initially attended school in Blackpool and later in Handsworth, Birmingham, where he enthused over a game of football, always wanting to get involved in the playground kick-about as well as joining other lads down the local park.

Berry had an unsuccessful trial with Ipswich Town before joining Wolves as an apprentice in April 1974, turning professional on his 18th birthday and making his League debut against Chelsea in the penultimate game of the 1976–77 season when both clubs were going at it hammer and tongue for the Second Division title. With regular defender John McAlle and his deputy Colin Brazier both sidelined, he was introduced into competitive soccer by manager Sammy Chung, who selected him alongside the experienced Frank Munro. He did well in front of the biggest crowd of the season – almost 33,500 – who witnessed the 1–1 draw, which in the end was enough to bring the Championship trophy to Molineux.

Berry made seven appearances the following season as Wolves re-established themselves in the top flight before gaining a regular place in the side alongside McAlle in 1978–79 – although, in truth, it was a tough campaign with relegation being avoided with three games remaining. During that season he won the first of five full caps for Wales, ironically against the country of his birth West Germany at Wrexham in a European Championship qualifier in May 1979 – becoming the second black player (behind Eddie Parris) to represent the principality. Unfortunately he was on the losing side (2–0). His other international appearances came against the Republic of Ireland, West Germany (again) and Turkey in 1979–80 and versus England in 1982–83 as a Stoke player.

Emlyn Hughes was signed from Liverpool at the start of the 1979–80 season, and he slotted in alongside Berry at the heart of the Wolves defence. The pair played superbly well together, and it turned out to be another excellent season for the Molineux club, who won the League Cup for the second time, beating Nottingham Forest 1–0 at Wembley, Berry putting the shackles on Forest's danger man Trevor Francis.

Injuries and suspension affected his performances over the next two years, and after a very uneasy 1981–82 campaign, which ended in relegation, Berry was transferred to Stoke City where he was reunited with his former playing colleague Derek Parkin and manager Sammy Chung. He appeared in 260 first-class matches for the Potters in eight years, some as captain, and scored 30 goals, a third of them from the penalty spot. He slowly drifted down the footballing ladder after 1990, and in later years, after returning to the Staffordshire area, he did a lot to promote soccer at various schools, youth clubs and pre-arranged functions, while also having his own programme on the local BBC radio station.

In the programme printed for his testimonial match in August 1990, former Wolves striker John Richards wrote this about George: '...Whether on the field or in the dressing room, George's infectious and audible enthusiasm was an example to any player young and old. A bit wearing on the eardrums, but he could not be faulted for his dedication and wholehearted commitment to the game.'

ALF BISHOP

Date of birth: 8 April 1886, Stourbridge, West Midlands
Died: 8 August 1938, Wolverhampton

Wolves record:
Appearances: League 357, FA Cup 25, Wartime 6
Goals: League 6, FA Cup 0, Wartime 0
Debut: League, 1 September 1906 v Hull City (h) drew 1–1

Also played for: Halesowen Town, Merthyr Town, Wrexham

Originally a composed, self-disciplined full-back in non-League football with Halesowen, Alf Bishop joined Wolves as a full-time professional in June 1905, and after spending a season in the reserves, where he was converted into a right-half, he made his League debut in that position on the opening day of the 1906–07 Second Division campaign against Hull City at Molineux.

Playing exceptionally well, Bishop retained his place in the side and eventually took over the centre-half spot from Billy Woodridge as Wolves battled in vain to gain promotion to the First Division, which they had vacated the previous season. He was switched to left-half halfway through the 1907–08 season, where he formed a wonderful middle-line trio alongside the Reverend Kenneth Hunt and Woodridge who was brought back into the side in the centre-forward position.

Wolves' form improved greatly, and with Bishop outstanding progress was made in the FA Cup competition. Some excellent performances resulted in the team reaching the Final for the fourth time in the club's history, and the match was played brilliantly in front of almost 75,000 spectators at Crystal Palace. Alf and his colleagues pulled out all the stops to beat the red-hot favourites Newcastle United 3–1 to lift the coveted trophy for the second time following the success in 1893. However, the main priority at this juncture was to regain their First Division status, but despite the drive, commitment, skill and endeavour of Bishop promotion eluded Wolves.

Bishop, who never shirked a tackle or, indeed, a challenge and always gave encouragement to his colleagues, continued to do the business on the field. Skippering the team on occasions, unfortunately he was not getting any younger, his legs were beginning to feel the pressure, and after guesting for Merthyr Town in 1917 and playing in the Victory League for Wolves in 1919 he chose to leave Molineux in May 1920, after more than 380 senior appearances for the club. He was signed by Wrexham but injuries started to catch up with him, and he took employment in a local department store before returning to Wolverhampton where he died in 1938, aged 52.

It was a crying shame that Alf, a totally committed footballer, never gained international recognition.

PAUL BRADSHAW

Date of birth:	28 April 1956, Altrincham, Cheshire
Wolves record:	
Appearances:	League 200, FA Cup 23, League Cup 18, Europe 2
Goals:	0
Debut:	League, 1 October 1977 v Leicester City (h) won 3–0
Also played for:	Blackburn Rovers, West Bromwich Albion (2 spells), Vancouver Whitecaps (NASL), Bristol Rovers, Newport County, Walsall, Peterborough United, England (4 Under-21 caps)

Paul Bradshaw represented Altrincham & Cheshire Boys and had a trail with Manchester United before joining Blackburn Rovers as an apprentice in January 1972, turning professional 18 months later. After making more than 80 senior appearances for the Ewood Park club, and gaining the first two of his four England Under-21 caps versus Wales and Scotland, he was transferred to Wolves for £150,000 in September 1977, manager Sammy Chung recruiting him to take over from Gary Pierce.

Tall, strong and agile with a safe pair of hands, Bradshaw was also courageous and a fine shot-stopper who would often fling himself at the feet of opposing forwards. He had his off days – as do all goalkeepers – but overall he proved to be an excellent signing by Wolves, for whom he appeared in 243 competitive games, helping the team win the League Cup at Wembley in 1980, playing against Nottingham Forest, and reach the FA Cup semi-final 12 months later, beaten by Tottenham Hotspur in a replay. He also gained two more Under-21 caps for his country, lining up against Finland and Yugoslavia in 1978–79.

In his first season at Molineux in 1977–78 Bradshaw, playing behind a defence that included full-backs Geoff Palmer and Derek Parkin, Colin Brazier, John McAlle and Bob Hazell, was active in 37 senior matches. The following season he missed only three League games, was absent on six occasions in 1979–80 and four times in 1980–81, before completing his only ever-present campaign in 1981–82 when, sadly, relegation was suffered to the Second Division. He was voted Wolves Player of the Year in both 1981 and 1982.

At this juncture, manager Ian Greaves gave way to Graham Hawkins, who immediately replaced Bradshaw with the experienced John Burridge, signed from Queen's Park Rangers. Promotion was subsequently gained (at the first attempt), but Bradshaw, disappointed of course at not being part of the triumphant team, was still playing second fiddle, and he had to fight his way back into the side, managing only 12 games in 1983–84 before being transferred to Vancouver Whitecaps in the NASL at the end of that campaign.

Bradshaw returned to Football League action with Wolves' arch rivals West Bromwich Albion in February 1985, acted as coach at Walsall for a short time, played briefly for Bristol Rovers and Newport County, had a second spell at The Hawthorns (1988–90) and rounded off an interesting career with Peterborough United, retiring in May 1991. Bradshaw later returned to Wolverhampton to work as a security officer. A member of the Wolves former Players' Association, he left the area a few years ago.

PETER BROADBENT

Date of birth:	15 May 1933, Elvington near Dover, Kent

Wolves record:

Appearances:	League 452, FA Cup 31, Europe 11, Others 3
Goals:	League 127, FA Cup 10, Europe 7, Others 1
Debut:	League, 17 March 1951 v Portsmouth (h) lost 3–2
Also played for:	Shrewsbury Town, Aston Villa, Stockport County, Bromsgrove Rovers, England (1 B, 1 Under-23 and 7 full caps)

Peter Broadbent, the son of a miner, was a record signing by Wolves when he joined the club as a 17-year-old from Brentford in February 1951 for £10,000. He admitted 'I jumped at the chance of joining Wolves. I wanted to better myself in the game, and I knew that the competition of trying to get into the first team when there were players in the side like Jesse Pye, Jimmy Dunn and Sammy Smyth was sure to be good for me. I aimed high to get high.' And he certainly reached the heights, there's no question about that.

Broadbent appeared in almost 500 senior games for the club, scored 145 goals, gained three League Championship-winning medals in the 1950s, won the FA Cup in 1960, played for England at B, Under-23 and senior levels (participating in the World Cup Finals in Sweden in 1958) and twice represented the Football League. He certainly deserved more honours but was unfortunate to have several other quality players to compete with for a place in the national team, including Johnny Haynes, Bobby Robson and even Bobby Charlton.

A hard-working, scheming, ball-playing midfielder who loved to drive forward and have a crack at goal, Broadbent made the Wolves side tick in the 1950s. An elegant, beautifully balanced player who preferred the inside-right position, he was a complete master on the ball and his passes, long or short, were inch-perfect. He used to pick out his wingers (Johnny Hancocks and Jimmy Mullen, and later Norman Deeley) with one 40–50 yard measured pass, changing defence into attack in an instant.

After gaining a regular place in the team in 1953, Peter remained a permanent fixture in manager Stan Cullis's side over the next 12 years. Indeed, his name was one of the first to be entered on the team sheet. He scored 12 goals in 36 appearances when the League title was won for the first time in 1954, netted 17 times in 40 outings when the Championship was won again in 1958 and added another 20 goals to his tally in 40 matches when Wolves secured the star prize for a third time in 1959.

Broadbent had the pleasure of scoring Wolves' first two goals in a major European tournament, doubling up against the German side FC Schalke '04 in the European Cup in November 1958 (2–2 draw), and, of course, he made his debut at international level, collecting his first senior cap against Russia in the 1958 World Cup Finals. Later that year he netted twice in England's 2–2 draw with Wales at Villa Park, and in 1959 he starred in a 1–0 win over Scotland at Wembley when his teammate Billy Wright won his 100th senior cap.

On Boxing Day 1964, when Wolves met Aston Villa, Broadbent said goodbye to the Molineux fans who had marvelled at his talents for 13 years. A month later he joined Shrewsbury Town, signed by former Wolves wartime player Arthur Rowley. After his spell at Gay Meadow he spent three years with Aston Villa (1966–69), had a season with Stockport County and ended his career with Bromsgrove Rovers. He later ran a successful babywear shop in Halesowen and lived in Codsall with his wife Shirley but is now sadly suffering from Alzheimer's disease.

To many Wolves fans (especially those who saw him play) Broadbent is regarded as the greatest-ever footballer to wear the club's colours. Besides being a superb footballer, he was also a champion golfer, and in 1968 he won the professional footballers' golf title, having finished runner-up in 1965 and 1966. He also won the Staffordshire Amateur Open title and nowadays his son Gary and grandson Andrew, who captured the World Boys' title in 2002, are both deeply involved in the small-ball game.

JOHN BRODIE

Date of birth:	30 August 1862, Wightwick near Wolverhampton
Died:	16 February 1925, Wolverhampton

Wolves record:

Appearances:	League 42, FA Cup 23
Goals:	League 22, FA Cup 22
Debut:	FA Cup, 27 October 1883 v Long Eaton Rangers (h) won 4–1
Also played for:	West Bromwich Albion (guest)

Educated, like so many other early Wolves players, at St Luke's School in Blakenhall, John Brodie was one of the founder-members of Wolverhampton Wanderers football Club in 1877, and while things were behind sorted out behind the scenes, fixtures being arranged, players signed and the ground sorted out, he attended Saltley College in Birmingham for two years (1880–82) before continuing his career in football.

Able to occupy a variety of positions but preferring the centre-forward berth, Brodie played in several local friendly matches and Cup ties before scoring twice on his senior debut for Wolves in a comprehensive 4–1 win over Long Eaton Rangers in a first-round FA Cup tie at Dudley Road in October 1883 – this being Wolves' first ever game in this acclaimed competition. He poached two more goals in his next FA Cup encounter against Wednesbury Old Athletic, which surprisingly Wolves lost 3–2, and by the time League football was introduced in September 1888 he had already notched 15 goals in that competition for Wolves alone, including his first major hat-trick, secured in a record-breaking 14–0 home victory over Crosswell's Brewery in November 1886.

Brodie made 13 appearances in the 1888–89 League campaign and struck 11 goals, including one in each of the nine successive games between 20 October and 22 December. He also played in four of the six FA Cup matches, helping Wolves reach the Final for the first time in the club's history. Alas, high-flying Preston North End, beaten finalists the previous season, proved the stronger team on the day and won 3–0 to clinch the double. However, it wasn't all doom and gloom for him that season, far from it. He twice represented England at senior level, scoring on his debut in a 6–1 win over Ireland at Goodison Park, and also featured prominently against Scotland in a 3–2 defeat at The Oval. He later added a third cap to his collection when, in 1891, he played left-half against Ireland, who were once again crushed 6–1, this time on his home pitch at Molineux.

Described in the local paper as being 'a penetrative forward', Brodie was well built, quick and strong with a powerful right-foot shot. He possessed a fair amount of skill, was hard working and 'a trier to the finish of a game.' He continued playing until the summer of 1891 when he retired with a knee injury, which had been troubling him for six months. In later life he had a pronounced limp... no doubt a legacy of his footballing days.

At that juncture (1891), Brodie took up refereeing, which he did on a part-time basis outside his duties as headmaster at St Peter's School, Wolverhampton. In August 1913, some 36 years after initially signing, and indeed, helping form the club, he was opted on to the board of directors at Molineux. Always a very popular and talkative person, he lightened up many a dull meeting with his witty and devilish remarks, his gentlemanly deportment often bringing smiles to the faces of his fellow directors! He remained on the board until the mid 1920s when he resigned to spend more time on his teaching.

SAMMY BROOKS

Date of birth:	28 March 1890, Brierley Hill, Staffordshire
Died:	13 January 1960, Brierley Hill, Staffordshire.

Wolves record:

Appearances:	League 224, FA Cup 22, Wartime 4
Goals:	League goals 50, FA Cup 3, Wartime 1
Debut:	League, 8 April 1910 v Bradford Park Avenue (h) drew 0–0
Also played for:	Brierley Hill Corinthians, Brierley Hill Alliance, Bilston United, Cradley Heath (two spells), Tottenham Hotspur, Southend United, Kidderminster Harriers, Stourbridge, England (1 Victory cap)

As a youngster, Sammy Brooks played local football in the Black Country, sometimes taking part in three matches a week, including two on a Saturday. He loved the game and at the age of 16 signed for Bilston United where he was spotted by Wolves who secured his services, initially as an amateur before handing him a professional contract in August 1910.

A darting, tricky left-winger, known as 'Little Giant', Brooks spent 12 excellent seasons at Molineux, during which time he averaged a goal every five games, appeared in the 1921 FA Cup Final at Stamford Bridge, was capped by England in a Victory international in 1919 and also represented the Football League versus the Irish League in October 1914. Within two years of turning 'pro' he had established himself in the first team, forming an excellent left-wing partnership with Jack Needham.

Standing at just 5ft 2in tall and weighing less than 9st, Brooks was certainly one of the shortest and lightest players ever to wear the famous gold and black strip, but he was always involved in the action, and he certainly enjoyed a challenge, often giving as good as he got when opposed by a rock-solid full-back – although, in truth, his pace helped him skip past his marker at will, and when tackled he was lithe and subtle enough to escape serious injury. He packed a decent left-foot shot and when given the chance crossed the ball accurately and at pace from the touchline.

After firmly establishing himself on the left flank Brooks hardly missed a game. He had his best season in terms of appearances in 1914–15 when he was absent from the side just once – a 2–0 defeat at Huddersfield when Dick Richards deputised. He also netted 18 goals that term – his best overall tally – and at the time it was the best return ever by an orthodox Wolves winger. Brooks had top scored the season before with 11 goals.

During the war Brooks played very little football until 1919 when the Midland Victory League was introduced. He was in good form and was selected to play against Wales at Cardiff in October of that year, lining up in the same forward line as the great Charlie Buchan and Syd Puddefoot. In the first season after the hostilities he had five different partners on the left wing but still produced some fine displays despite Wolves struggling in the lower reaches of the Second Division. The following year he once again performed admirably as Wolves swept away all before them to reach the Cup Final. Unfortunately, on a tacky, wet Chelsea pitch, they lost 1–0 to Tottenham Hotspur, the team Brooks would join 15 months later.

Switched to the right-wing by secretary-manager Jack Addenbrooke who wanted to accommodate fresh players, Brooks struggled with injury during the 1921–22 season, and when George Jobey took charge of the team he was transferred to Spurs, where he joined forces with another impish footballer, 'Fanny' Walden, who was only an inch taller. Sadly he was a huge disappointment at White Hart Lane, and in May 1924, after making just 16 appearances, he was signed for Southend United, later assisting three Midlands clubs, one being his former employers Cradley Heath. He retired in May 1927. His brother, Ernie, played for Blackburn Rovers, Wolves reserves and Brierley Hill.

MAJOR FRANK BUCKLEY

Date of birth: 9 November 1882, Urmston, Manchester
Died: 22 December 1964, Walsall

Wolves record:
Manager: July 1927 to March 1944

Played for: Aston Villa, Brighton & Hove Albion, Manchester United, Manchester City, Birmingham, Derby County, Bradford City, Norwich City, England (1 cap)
Also managed: Norwich City, Blackpool, Notts County, Hull City, Leeds United, Walsall

Unfortunately Major Frank Buckley's sides never won a major honour – Wolves came close to completing the League and FA Cup double in 1939, finishing runners-up in both competitions, and lifted the 1942 Wartime League Cup – yet he was one of the most famous managers in the history of the game.

The Major won fame as a shrewd dealer in the transfer market, especially during his 17-year reign at Molineux. People said he was ahead of his time, but his patriarchal, disciplined approach seemed to suit the era in which he managed.

In 1898 Buckley joined the Army and after serving in the Boer War became a professional footballer with Aston Villa in 1903. Playing at centre-half, he appeared in 165 League games for seven different clubs and gained his only England cap versus Ireland in 1914 before becoming a Commanding Officer in the Footballers' Battalion (Middlesex Regiment). After his demob in 1919 he became player-manger of Southern League side Norwich City, but following a crisis within the club, which resulted in six directors resigning, he too quit the Nest (Norwich's ground at the time).

Out of the game for three years, during which time he worked as a commercial traveller, Buckley returned to football management with Blackpool, then took the hot seat at Molineux in May 1927 when he succeeded Fred Scotchbrook. Immediately he began to turn young unknowns into stars, and in 1932 Wolves regained their First Division status after trying for 26 years. Keeping the directors happy, he signed and developed some brilliant players including Stan Cullis, Dennis Westcott, Jimmy Mullen, Bryn Jones and a certain Billy Wright, although at first he didn't think Wright was tall or strong enough to become a footballer and sent him away to build up his strength.

Over a period of four years, from 1935 to 1939, Wolves received a massive £10,658 in transfer fees (big money in those days), and it was all due to the Major's inspired dealings in the transfer market. However, with things going extremely well on the pitch, it came as a body blow, especially to him, when the team surprisingly lost 4–1 to underdogs Portsmouth in the 1939 FA Cup Final and also missed out on winning their first ever League Championship in the same month.

Capturing the Wartime Football League Cup in 1942 was no consolation, and two years later the club chairman Ben Matthews had retired, and the Major also left Molineux, admitting that he was now 'feeling vulnerable'.

Some of the Major's methods were certainly controversial, like his 'monkey gland injections' which, in effect, were simply inoculations against colds. He also sent players to see a psychologist in his search for that elusive self-confidence boost, and he would often arrange for the pitch to be watered prior to a Wolves home game – simply because he loved playing on soft ground.

The Major remained in football until he was almost 72 years of age, spending his last two seasons with Walsall prior to his retirement in September 1955. He was associated with the game for more than half a century.

Major Buckley had five brothers, one of whom, Chris, played for Aston Villa as well as Arsenal, and was chairman at Villa Park from 1955 to 1966.

STEVE BULL, MBE

Date of birth: 28 March 1965, Tipton, West Midlands

Wolves record:
Appearances: League 461+13, FA Cup 18+2, League Cup 32+1, Others 34
Goals: League 250, FA Cup 7, League Cup 18, Others 31
Debut: League, 22 November 1986 v Wrexham (h) lost 3–0

Also played for: Tipton Town, West Bromwich Albion, Hereford United, England (5 Under-21, 5 B and 13 caps)

The greatest goalscorer in the long and eventful history of Wolverhampton Wanderers football club, Steve Bull played for his school teams, Ocker Hill Infants and Willingsworth High, as well as two local junior teams, Red Lion and Newey Goodman, before joining Tipton Town. His goalscoring expertise was noted by West Bromwich Albion, and after a series of talks he signed professional forms at The Hawthorns in August 1985.

Bull scored three goals in nine games for the Baggies before transferring to Wolves in November 1986, along with Andy Thompson, in a combined deal worth £70,000, Steve being valued at £50,000. 'Bully', as he became known to every Wolves supporter, made his debut against Wrexham 48 hours later in front 5,252 fans. The team were struggling in the Fourth Division at the time, and Molineux was a very depressing place to be. Worse was to come when on the following Monday evening Cup-tied 'Bully' sat in the stand and watched as Wolves suffered the worst humiliation in their history by crashing out of the FA Cup to non-League Chorley. He was straight back into the team after that disaster, and he scored the first of his 306 goals for Wolves in a Freight Rover Trophy game at Cardiff, following up with his first in the League to earn a 1–0 victory at Hartlepool.

Bull claimed five more goals up to February 1987, when Wolves met Stockport at Molineux, a game many people saw as the turning point for the club. Trailing 1–0 with 14 minutes to go, Wolves suddenly clicked into gear and scored three times to win the game, Steve netting once. Only three of the remaining 22 games that season ended in defeats, and amazingly Wolves just missed out on promotion, losing to Aldershot in the Play-off Final. In 1986–87 he scored 19 goals, including his first hat-trick for the club in a 4–1 win over Hartlepool.

Already with many admirers, in 1987–88 Bull became a hero as Wolves won the Fourth Division Championship and beat Burnley 2–0 to lift the Sherpa Van Trophy at Wembley. That season he scored 52 times, 34 in the League, making him the first player to claim half a century of goals in a season of English football since Peterborough's Terry Bly almost 30 years earlier. The following season he netted four hat-tricks and two four-timers in another 50-goal haul as Wolves won the Third Division title and came within a whisker of returning to Wembley. And for the record, the last player to score 50 goals in successive seasons was Middlesbrough's George Camsell in the mid 1920s.

Bull's marksmanship brought him international recognition, being capped by England for the first time against Scotland at Hampden Park in May 1989, scoring in a 2–1 win. The following April he netted twice against Czechoslovakia to clinch a place in the squad for the World Cup Finals in Italy. He won 13 full caps in total, eight of them as a substitute, and scored four goals. He also played in five B and five Under-21 internationals.

In March 1992 Bull broke the Wolves scoring record set by John Richards when he netted his 195th goal playing Derby County, and he remained loyal to the club by resisting the temptation to join a team in the Premiership. In February 1998 he scored his 300th goal for Wolves, following up six months later with his record-breaking 18th hat-trick.

Unfortunately a tedious knee injury failed to respond to surgery, and in the summer of 1999, at the age of 35, 'Bully' quit top-line soccer. He joined the Conference side Hereford United the following season but didn't play much, retiring to concentrate on his work at Molineux in a PR capacity. He still turns out in the ex-players team in charity matches.

He was awarded the MBE in the Millennium New Year's honours list for services to football.

WILLIE CARR

Date of birth: 6 January 1950, Glasgow

Wolves record:
Appearances: League 231+6, FA Cup 28+1, League Cup 21, Europe 2
Goals: League 21, FA Cup 4, League Cup 1, Europe 0
Debut: League, 15 March 1975 v Chelsea (h) won 7–1

Also played for: Coventry City, Millwall, Worcester City, Willenhall Town, Stourbridge, Scotland (4 Under-23, 6 full caps)

William Mclanny Carr was educated in Cambridge and was the star of Coventry City's 1968 youth team before developing into a skilful, enterprising midfielder who went on to score 37 goals in 298 competitive games for the Sky Blues before joining Wolves for a knockdown price of £80,000 in March 1975, when the Highfield Road club's financial position was very precarious. Twelve months prior to his move Wolves boss Bill McGarry had offered £240,000 for his services but pulled out of the deal when the player failed a medical. He had severely injured his knee at Liverpool in April 1973 when only 23, and it took quite a while for him to recover. At one time he was under intense daily treatment, and he played in only 13 League games the following season. Thankfully all was well in the end, and he continued to perform superbly well for Wolves, whom he served for seven years, up to August 1982 when he was transferred to Millwall.

Carr, who was a tireless worker, had flare, ability, vision, skill, aggression and could pass a ball with great precision. He was able to manufacture openings out of nothing for his strikers, and he certainly contributed greatly when Wolves won the Second Division Championship in 1977 and the League Cup in 1980.

Replacing Steve Daley in midfield, Carr made a terrific start to his Wolves career, scoring on his debut in an emphatic 7–1 home League win over Chelsea. He appeared in the last 10 games of that season and 35 in 1975–76 when, sadly, Wolves were relegated. But along with fellow midfielders Daley, Kenny Hibbitt and Martin Patching, among others, he played with gusto and commitment as Wolves regained their top-flight status at the first attempt, Willie weighing in with four goals, including crucial ones against Sheffield United (2–2) and Nottingham Forest (won 2–1).

Between 1977 and 1980 Carr continued to do the business and missed only 14 games out of a possible 126 in the League as Wolves re-established themselves among the big boys and went to Wembley, where they lifted the League Cup for the second time in six years by beating Nottingham Forest 1–0.

Manager John Barnwell and his replacement Ian Greaves kept faith with the red-haired Scotsman for another two seasons, during which time Wolves were beaten by Arsenal in the FA Cup semi-final of 1981. But then, after Graham Hawkins had taken charge, he moved on to pastures new. He didn't have the happiest of times with Millwall and within six months had moved into non-League football with Worcester City. A succession of moves around the West Midlands, which included a spell as player-manager of Willenhall Town, culminated with a season at Stourbridge before he finally hung up his boots in 1988.

Carr, who was part of that infamous 'donkey-kick' routine involving the former Wolves player Ernie Hunt when playing for Coventry City against Everton in October 1970, won the first of his six full caps for Scotland against Northern Ireland in 1969 and the last in 1972 versus Peru. He would surely have gained more senior honours had he been with a bigger club than Coventry, with whom he won all his senior caps, but he nevertheless did an excellent job for his clubs and also for his country.

Willie now lives in Shropshire.

EDDIE CLAMP

Date of birth: 14 September 1934, Coalville, Leicestershire
Died: 10 November 1995, Wolverhampton

Wolves record:
Appearances: League 214, FA Cup 14, Europe 9
Goals: League 23, FA Cup 2, Europe 0
Debut: 6 March 1954 v Manchester United (a) lost 1–0.

Also played for: Arsenal, Stoke City, Peterborough United, Worcester City, Lower Gornal, England (4 caps)

A pupil at Bridge Road Secondary School, Coalville, Eddie Clamp represented both Leicestershire and England schoolboys before joining Wolves as an amateur early in 1950. After impressing the Molineux coaching staff and, indeed, his manager Stan Cullis, he was taken on the professional staff in April 1952 and made his Football League debut against Manchester United in front of 39,000 spectators at Old Trafford almost two years later – the first of 241 senior appearances for the club.

At the time of his debut Wolves were battling it out with neighbours West Bromwich Albion for the First Division title, and at the end of the season a delighted Clamp, although appearing in only two games, duly celebrated victory with his teammates. Having to fight for his place in the team, simply because Wolves were blessed with quality half-backs in the 1950s, Bill Slater, Ron Flowers, Billy Wright to name just three, he made only 11 senior appearances in 1954–55 but upped his tally to 28 the following season when he became an established member of the first-team squad.

However, Clamp spent three-quarters of 1956–57 in the reserves before bedding down at right-half in place of Bill Slater for the 1957–58 campaign, when Wolves performed splendidly to register their second League Championship triumph in four years, Eddie missing only one game, the last against Sheffield Wednesday. He also netted 10 goals, including a vital strike in a 3–2 win at Leicester, the only one of the game at home to Portsmouth and a late penalty to earn a point from a 1–1 draw in the Black Country derby with Albion at Molineux.

Clamp – who was nicknamed 'Chopper' by the fans – was a strong and resolute player with a crunching tackle. He had been in outstanding form for two years; so much so, that he was called into England's World Cup squad by manager Walter Winterbottom, who handed him his international debut against Russia before the 1958 Finals in Sweden. He was then selected in three games in the tournament proper versus Russia, Brazil and Austria, when his two half-back colleagues were his Molineux buddies Billy Wright and Bill Slater. Another Wolves star Peter Broadbent was also in the squad.

Adding a second League Championship-winners' medal to his collection in 1958–59, when he shared the right-half berth with Slater and also filled in on the left flank for Flowers, Clamp continued to impress at club level, and a year on he helped Wolves beat Blackburn Rovers 3–0 in the 1960 FA Cup Final. That success was followed with another fine season from Clamp as Wolves finished third in the League, but then, four months into the 1961–62 campaign, he was replaced by Johnny Kirkham. In November 1961 he was sold to Arsenal for £34,000, and in September 1962, after making 24 appearances for the Gunners, he was sold by his former teammate Billy Wright to Stoke City for £12,000. The recipient of a Second Division Championship medal with the Potters in his first season at The Victoria Ground, he went on to assist Peterborough United before entering non-League football with Worcester City in 1965, retiring two years later. Thereafter, he ran his own business and was a regular visitor to Molineux right up until his untimely death at the age of 61.

Eddie's mother was employed as the laundry lady at Molineux for a number of years.

NEW
RY

WAYNE CLARKE

Date of birth: 28 February 1961, Willenhall

Wolves record:
Appearances: League 130+19, FA Cup 9+2, League Cup 8+2, Europe 0+1
Goals: League 30, FA Cup 1, League Cup 2, Europe 0
Debut: League, 16 September 1978 v Ipswich Town (h) lost 3–1

Also played for: Birmingham City, Everton, Leicester City, Manchester City, Shrewsbury Town (two spells), Stoke City, Walsall, Telford United
Managed: Telford United

One of five footballing brothers (the others being England international Allan, Derek, Frank and Kelvin) striker Wayne Clarke played for England at Schoolboy and Youth-team levels and also represented the West Midlands Schools as a teenager. He joined Wolves as a 15-year-old in June 1976, and after developing through the intermediate and reserve teams he signed as a full-time professional at Molineux in March 1978.

Although Mel Eves, John Richards and Billy Rafferty were ahead of him in the pecking order for a place in the first-team forward line, Clarke was given his League debut (in place of Rafferty) by manager Sammy Chung against Ipswich Town at Molineux in September 1978, following a run of four defeats in five games and only four goals scored. Wolves lost 3–1 to the FA Cup holders, but he kept his place for the next game at Everton and went on to have a further six outings in the senior side that season, including his first in the FA Cup at home to Newcastle United. He also scored his first League goal – helping his team earn a point from a 3–3 draw at QPR.

When Wolves added Andy Gray to their strike force at the start of the 1979–80 season, it looked as though Clarke's chances of first-team action would be restricted even more. But he stuck in there and played in 16 competitive games that term, watching from the stand at Wembley as Wolves won the League Cup. Norman Bell then came along to boost Wolves' attacking options even further, but Clarke remained loyal to the club and was given 22 outings by manager John Barnwell during the 1980–81 campaign and 26 the following season when, alas, Wolves were relegated to the Second Division.

With another new manager at the helm in Graham Hawkins, Clarke became the first choice in 1982–83 as promotion was achieved at the first attempt. Playing alongside Gray and Eves, and sometimes Billy Livingstone, he scored 12 goals, most of them from inside the penalty-area. But he was no poacher, he was quick, had good footwork and packed a powerful right-foot shot, often trying his luck from distance. He was also a decent header of the ball.

Sadly 1983–84 proved to be another disappointing season for Clarke and Wolves as the team slipped back into the Second Division. At that point he was transferred to Birmingham City for £80,000. After scoring 43 goals in 105 games for Blues, he signed for Everton for £500,000 in March 1987, teaming up at Goodison Park with his former Molineux colleague Andy Gray.

Clarke helped the Merseysiders win the League Championship in his first season and then scored the winning goal in the Charity Shield game at Wembley against Coventry City before moving to Leicester City in July 1989. Six months later he switched his allegiance to Manchester City in another £500,000 deal, and after loan spells with Shrewsbury Town, Stoke City and Wolves (September 1991, when he partnered Steve Bull in the game at Southend) he quit Maine Road to join Kenny Hibbitt's Walsall (August 1992). He then spent another two seasons with Shrewsbury (gaining a Third Division winners' medal in 1994) before becoming player-manager of Telford United, resigning his position in November 1996. He ended his senior career with a record of 151 goals in 511 competitive games and later became a postman.

BILLY CROOK

Date of birth: 7 June 1926, Wolverhampton

Wolves record:
Appearances: League 196, FA Cup 24, Other 1, Wartime 121
Goals: League 2, FA Cup 1, Other 0, Wartime 6
Debut: War Cup (League), 10 January 1942 v Blackpool (a) lost 6–1

Also played for: Boulton & Paul FC, Walsall, Wellington Town

Billy Crook was a part-time player at Molineux, earning his keep in two ways – as a footballer with Wolves and as a structural draughtsman with the local engineering company Rubery Owen & Co. (Darlaston), for whom he worked full-time after retiring from the game at the age of 34.

Spotted playing in the local junior League, Crook joined Wolves as a 14-year-old in August 1940 and signed amateur forms in July 1941 after leaving grammar school. He developed his game during the war and eventually became a part-time professional in August 1943. A guest player for Aldershot and Chelsea during the hostilities, he made over 120 wartime appearances for Wolves before League football recommenced in August 1946. At that juncture, he was already an established member of the side and missed only three games in that initial post World War Two campaign as Wolves finished third in Division One. The following season he appeared in 31 League games and 36 in 1948–49 when Wolves went all the way to the FA Cup Final.

Crook, a very confident and stylish footballer with a solid frame and neat tricks, played at right-half alongside Bill Shorthouse and Billy Wright – and there was no doubt that Wolves had a very capable middle line around this time. He played very well at Wembley as Wolves overcame a plucky Leicester City outfit by 3–1 to lift the trophy for the third time in their history and the first since 1908.

Wolves manager Stan Cullis certainly admired Crook as a player, describing him in one interview as being 'Highly-skilled, constructive, technical and a model of precision, whose many attributes included those of consistency and sportsmanship. There was nothing untidy about his play whatsoever.'

Crook continued to perform with great determination and conviction and made 41 senior appearances in 1949–50 followed by 27 and 20 respectively in the next two campaigns. Early in the 1952–53 season he lost his place to Ron Flowers, and with Bill Baxter acting as reserve half-back he knew his time was up – although he still maintained a high level of performance in the second XI despite carrying a few niggling injuries. He finally left Molineux in October 1954, travelling the short distance across the Black Country to nearby Walsall where he remained for two years, taking off his boots for good in 1960 after a spell in non-League football.

Crook was awarded a benefit in September 1950 after 10 years' dedicated service to the club, and, besides loving and enjoying football, he was also keen on Dixieland jazz and would travel miles to watch and listen to a quality group playing his kind of music. A member of the Wolves ex-players' association, he now lives in Cheshire. His brother, Alf Crook, also played for Wolves between 1942 and 1949.

STAN CULLIS

Date of birth:	25 October 1916, Ellesmere Port, Cheshire
Died:	27 February 2001, Malvern

Wolves record:

Appearances:	League 152, FA Cup 19, Wartime 34
Goals:	League 0, FA Cup 0, Wartime 0
Debut:	League, 16 February 1935 v Huddersfield Town (a) lost 3–2
Manager:	1948 to 1964
Also played for:	Bolton Wanderers (amateur), Ellesmere Port Wednesday and as a World War Two guest for Aldershot, Fulham and Liverpool, England (12 full and 20 Wartime/Victory caps)
Also managed:	Birmingham City

Stan Cullis served Wolves as a player and manager for 30 years, and there's no doubt that he was largely responsible for the team's success on the field during the 1950s when he was regarded, by many, as the best manager in the country.

As a player, occupying the right-half and centre-half positions, Cullis was a powerful tackler, strong in the air, who tried to hold the ball until he could use it and then, if possible, deliver a defence-splitting pass or perhaps take it through with his ungainly, crouching, dribbling style. Very rarely did he lose possession, but if he did he was quick to regain his defensive position. And not only did he perform superbly well for Wolves, he did likewise for England, gaining 32 caps in total, captaining the team at the age of 22 in a match against Romania in Bucharest in 1939. In fact, during the war he formed part of a magnificent England half-back line with Cliff Britton and Joe Mercer. He also played for the Football League on three occasions and starred in several representative matches when serving in the Army.

After making his Wolves debut in 1935, Cullis had to wait until the second half of the 1936–37 season before finally establishing himself in the first team, taking over from Bill Morris at centre-half. He skippered Wolves for several years and led them at Wembley in the 1939 FA Cup Final, which unfortunately they lost 4–1 to Portsmouth. This was a big disappointment, but he certainly made up for this set-back with some great achievements as a manager.

Cullis missed only eight League games in the last two campaigns before World War Two and then, during the hostilities, made 34 appearances in regional competitions before continuing at senior level in 1946–47 when Wolves finished third in Division One. At the end of that season Stan, who was now prone to concussive injuries, announced his retirement as a player to become assistant to manager Ted Vizard, and when Vizard parted company with the club a year later he took charge of the team.

As a manager Cullis instilled a fighting quality into his players and built a side that thrived on the quick, long pass – some even called it the big boot. It worked wonders as Wolves, playing a unique brand of direct, robust football and stretching their opponents with wing-to-wing crosses, packed Molineux for most home games.

Ten years after losing a Cup Final, Cullis was a winner in 1949 when Wolves beat Leicester City 3–1. Five years later he guided the club to its first-ever League Championship and followed up with two more Division One triumphs in 1958 and 1959 and a second Cup success in 1960. In between times he saw Wolves beat the cream of Europe (including Honved, Moscow Spartak, Moscow Dynamo and Real Madrid) in high-profile, floodlit games at Molineux, and above all he signed and developed some terrific footballers. Alas, things started to go wrong in 1961, and although he tried his best to get things back on track he was sacked in September 1964. His dismissal led to bitter recriminations from fans and the media alike. How could a man who had served his club so well for so long be so shabbily treated? That question was never answered.

For the next 15 months Cullis worked as a sales representative for the Coventry City chairman Derrick Robbins before becoming manager of Birmingham City in December 1965. He remained at St Andrew's until March 1970, having taken the Blues to the semi-finals of both the League Cup in 1967 and FA Cup in 1968. He also signed Trevor Francis! After ending his football career, Stan, who by now was residing in Malvern, took a job with a travel agency and wrote a column for the Wolverhampton-based *Sporting Star*. He was 85 when he died.

HUGH CURRAN

Date of birth: 25 September 1943, Carstairs, Glasgow

Wolves record:
Appearances: League 77+5, FA Cup 2, League Cup 4, Europe 1+1, Others 7+1
Goals: League 40, FA Cup 0, League Cup 2, Europe 0, Others 5
Debut: League, 1 February 1969 v Burnley (h) drew 1–1

Also played for: Manchester United (apprentice), Shamrock Rovers, Third Lanark, Millwall, Corby Town, Norwich City, Oxford United (2 spells), Bolton Wanderers, Scotland (5 caps)

A determination to score goals continually made striker Hugh Curran venture to go in 'where it hurt' as the saying goes. He was quite fearless, had an abundance of attacking flair and possessed a strong left-foot shot. Despite having five cartilage operations in 10 years, his brave efforts in the Football League – which covered a period of 15 years from 1964 to 1979 when he was forced to retire through injury – brought him 164 goals in 403 appearances. And if you were to add his record in Cup competitions to those figures, his overall statistics were even more impressive: 184 goals in 462 matches.

Released by Manchester United, Curran gained some experience with the Irish club Shamrock Rovers before spending two tough years with Third Lanark as a semi-professional, where he hardly got a look in. Spotted by Millwall manager Billy Gray, he signed a full contract with the Londoners in March 1964 and stayed at The Den for almost two years. He then served Norwich City from January 1966 until January 1969 when Wolves boss Bill McGarry splashed out £60,000 for his signature – signed to aide and abet Irish international centre-forward Derek Dougan and, of course, to help boost the team's goal count.

Curran did both of those jobs pretty well, netting four times in his first 10 games and top-scoring with 23 goals in the League and Cup the following season (the fifth highest marksman in Division One). He then added a further 20 to his tally in 1970–71 when he helped the team win the Texaco Cup against Hearts.

In November 1969 Curran collected the first of his five full caps for Scotland, playing alongside Alan Gilzean in a 2–0 defeat by Austria in Vienna. His other international outings followed against Northern Ireland, England, Denmark and Russia in 1970–71, and he had the pleasure of scoring in a 3–1 reverse at Wembley.

With John Richards ready to make his mark in the Wolves attack, Curran suddenly found himself out of favour and he made only five starts, plus three substitute appearances in 1971–72, one coming in the second leg of the UEFA Cup Final, which Wolves lost 3–2 on aggregate to Tottenham Hotspur. That, in fact, was Hugh's last game for the club, and in September 1972 manager McGarry sold him to Oxford United for £50,000.

Curran became one of Oxford's best-loved players, making a massive impact in his first season at The Manor Ground when he scored 17 goals in 37 appearances (seven coming in his first five outings). He went on to net a total of 32 in 80 games for the U's before switching his allegiance, in a £40,000 deal, to Bolton Wanderers in September 1974, returning to Oxford for a second spell in July 1977. He remained at The Manor Ground until his retirement, appearing in his last League game in September 1978 just before his 35th birthday. He immediately returned to his native Carstairs where he ran his own hairdressing business and also looked after a string of grocery shops before becoming a licensee in Chorlton-cum-Studley. He later took over a well-established hotel in Lanarkshire.

STEVE DALEY

Date of birth: 15 April 1953, Barnsley

Wolves record:
Appearances: League 191+21, FA Cup 18+1, League Cup 5+1, Europe 3+3, Other 1
Goals: League 38, FA Cup 3, League Cup 0, Europe 2, Other 0
Debut: League, 25 September 1971, substitute v Nottingham Forest (h) won 4–2

Also played for: Manchester City, Seattle Sounders (NASL), San Diego Sockers (NASL), Walsall, Lye Town, Kettering Town, Old Wulfrunians, England (6 B caps)
Managed: Telford United, Bromsgrove Rovers, Bilston Town

On 5 September 1979 Yorkshire-born midfielder Steve Daley became the most expensive footballer in Britain when he joined Manchester City from Wolves for £1,437,500. This beat the previous transfer record by more than £400,000, Trevor Francis having switched from Birmingham City to Nottingham Forest seven months earlier for a shade over £1m.

Highly rated as a youngster, the fair-haired Daley signed for Wolves as an apprentice at the age of 16 and turned professional in June 1971. Four months later, after some impressive displays in the intermediate and reserve teams, he made his League debut as a substitute in place of Mike O'Grady against Nottingham Forest, scoring on his first start against Southampton a fortnight later. He also entered Europe for the first time during this season, helping Wolves beat Carl Zeiss Jena in East Germany to reach the quarter-finals of the UEFA Cup.

Daley was a semi-regular in the League team in 1973–74, and what a year it turned out to be for Wolves, who reached Wembley for the first time since 1960, beating Manchester City 2–1 to win the League Cup. Steve, though, didn't take part in the Final. He was in reserve, the central-midfield trio being skipper Mike Bailey, Kenny Hibbitt and Alan Sunderland, with Dave Wagstaffe the wide man on the left.

In 1974–75 Daley made 24 appearances and another 36 the following season when Wolves were relegated to the Second Division. At that juncture, manager Sammy Chung changed things around and started the new campaign with Daley on the right side of midfield. He enjoyed every minute of the next eight months as Wolves powered through to win the Second Division title at the first attempt, Steve being an ever present, contributing 13 vital League goals at home to Charlton, Southampton, Millwall, Fulham (2), Blackpool, Bristol Rovers and Notts County and away at Nottingham Forest, Hereford, Bristol Rovers, Oldham and Cardiff.

Daley continued his good form over the next two seasons, missing very few League games, although he was bitterly disappointed when Wolves lost to Arsenal in the semi-final of the FA Cup. He scored on his outing for Wolves in a 3–2 defeat by Manchester United at Old Trafford in May 1979, but his next appearance on a football pitch was back in Manchester, for City against Southampton at Maine Road, just 72 hours after leaving Molineux.

Daley spent less than two years with Manchester City (appearing in only 54 games) and after a spell in the NASL returned to England to sign for Burnley (November 1983). Following a second summer in America, he tasted his last League action with Walsall (1985–86) and after leaving the Saddlers slowly wound down his career in non-League circles as a player and then manager, the latter after he had worked briefly for a Midland-based brewery. He is now living in the South Staffs area.

Steve's father Alan was also a professional footballer, serving Mansfield Town, Hull City, Doncaster Rovers, Scunthorpe United, Stockport County, Crewe Alexandra and Coventry City between 1946 and 1961.

PETER DANIEL

Date of birth: 12 December 1955, Hull

Wolves record:
Appearances: League 157, FA Cup 19, League Cup 17, Europe 1
Goals: League 13, FA Cup 1, League Cup 2, Europe 0
Debut: League, 19 August 1978 v Aston Villa (a) lost 1–0

Also played for: Hull City, Minnesota Kicks (NASL), Sunderland, Lincoln City, Burnley, England (7 Under-21 caps)

Peter Daniel, who played at right-back early in his career, was the driving force in midfield for Wolves for six seasons, during which time he made almost 200 senior appearances. Signed on schoolboy forms by Hull City in 1969, he became an apprentice two years later and, after giving up his painting job, turned professional in September 1973.

After 134 outings for the Tigers, as well as gaining seven England Under-21 caps, Daniel joined Wolves for £82,000 in May 1978, making an immediate impact with his determination, commitment and intelligent and mobile style. He made his debut in the Midlands derby at Villa Park on the opening day of the 1978–79 season, when he partnered Geoff Palmer at full-back, but after half-a-dozen games in the number-two shirt he was pushed forward into midfield by manager Sammy Chung, where he linked up with Kenny Hibbitt and Willie Carr. His initial League season at Molineux was tough as Wolves finished 18th in the First Division. But in the FA Cup it was a different story... that is until the semi-final stage when Wolves lost 2–0 to Arsenal. This was a huge disappointment for him, and he believed that Wolves, despite their indifferent League form, could have won the trophy.

John Barnwell, who had taken over as manager in November 1979, was a great admirer of Daniel, once declaring 'He will run through a brick wall if he had to – he's totally committed – a grand player to have around.'

Daniel, who grew a beard to look more fearsome than he really was, missed only seven League games in his first two campaigns with Wolves. He netted some cracking goals, most of them struck with power and accuracy from a distance, his efforts against QPR, Leeds and Birmingham City in 1978–79 and Everton and Manchester City the following season all gaining vital points.

In 1979–80 Wolves edged up to sixth place in the League table as well as reaching the League Cup Final, where they took on, and beat, Nottingham Forest 1–0. Daniel, who scored a vital away goal in the first leg of the semi-final at Swindon, was outstanding at Wembley, and his long punt downfield led to the winning goal, tapped home by Andy Gray after a mix up between England 'keeper Peter Shilton and Dave Needham.

In February 1981 Daniel broke his leg in a League game against Aston Villa, forcing him to miss the FA Cup semi-final defeat by Arsenal (another blow). Thankfully he regained full fitness and was back in the side at the start of the new campaign which, sadly, was to end in relegation. That was another disappointment for him (and Wolves), but all was not lost, and with Graham Hawkins now in charge promotion was gained at the first attempt, although, due to injury, Daniel himself was confined to only 13 outings.

At this juncture, Daniel's position in the team was under threat, and after appearing in half of the fixtures in 1983–84 when, for a second time in three years, Wolves were relegated, he moved to Minnesota Kicks (May 1984), later returning to League action with Sunderland (August 1985) before winding down his career with Lincoln City and Burnley. He retired in May 1988 with almost 400 League appearances under his belt and is now living in his native Hull.

JIMMY DEACON

Date of birth: 23 January 1906, Glasgow
Died: c.1984, Scotland

Wolves record:
Appearances: League 149, FA Cup 9
Goals: League 52, FA Cup 4
Debut: League, 7 September 1929 v Bradford City (a) drew 2–2

Also played for: Darlington, Southend United, Hartlepools United

Jimmy Deacon was a key player in the Wolves team between 1929 and 1934, during which time he averaged a goal every three matches. Born to Irish parents in Glasgow, he was a lively inside-forward who could also lead the attack. He worked as a fitter before starting his League career in the north of England with Darlington, making two Third Division North appearances. He moved to Molineux at the age of 20, signed for a mere £250 by Major Frank Buckley who saw him as the right player to link up with the prolific Billy Hartill in the Wolves attack.

Standing at just 5ft 7in tall and weighing barely 11 stones, Deacon was certainly not the biggest or, indeed, the strongest of forwards, but he always gave a good, honest account himself when playing against sturdy and rugged defenders. He was quick over the ground, had good skills and a splendid body-swerve, but above all he was a sharp-shooter who packed a fierce right-foot shot and often fired the ball at goal from anything up to 30 yards. He was also clever at sneaking in on the blind side of a defender – and it is a fact that at least half of his goals came from inside the penalty-area. Quite often the diminutive player was applauded by fans and teammates alike for some great ball jugglery.

Deacon scored on his debut to earn a point at Bradford and generally did well in his first season of Second Division football, claiming nine goals as Wolves finished ninth in the table. The following term he virtually doubled his goal count as the team missed out on promotion by seven points after drawing five and losing two of their last nine League games, thus allowing neighbours West Bromwich Albion to take the runners'-up spot behind Everton with Tottenham Hotspur third.

With Bill Bottrill in the attack (in place of Forshaw) and with Hartill and Jimmy himself banging in the goals from all angles, Wolves at last regained their top-flight status in 1931–32, winning the Second Division title by two points from Leeds United after a splendid season. Injured early in that campaign, he came back strongly and played his part in a terrific team performance that saw four players reach double figures in the scoring stakes, Jimmy netting 13 times. He was in superb form when Bury and Port Vale were defeated 6–0 and 7–1 respectively in the space of eight days in early December, and later on he had a hand in four of the goals when Bradford Park Avenue were whipped 6–0 at Molineux.

Deacon started off well in the First Division, scoring seven goals in the opening 11 games, and with Hartill also in excellent scoring form Wolves seemed as though they would hold their own. But things started to go wrong and instead of them being a mid-table team they quickly skipped down the ladder into the relegation zone, eventually scrambling clear to finish in 20th place. Between them the players scored 80 League goals but conceded 96.

Changes were made in the defence and extra forwards were also introduced, so much so that Deacon made only eight appearances in 1933–34 when 15th place was claimed. Six weeks into the new season he was transferred to Southend United, having lost his place in the front line to Welshman Bryn Jones.

Deacon became more of a schemer, a creator of chances, with the Shrimpers, for whom he notched three goals in 100 Third Division South games before ending his career with Hartlepools United in 1938–40. After the war, he returned to Glasgow where he worked in industry as well as running a pub.

Jimmy's brother, Richard Deacon, also played for Wolves (1930–31) and West Ham United.

NORMAN DEELEY

Date of birth: 30 November 1933, Wednesbury, Staffordshire

Wolves record:
Appearances: League 206, FA Cup 16, Europe 12, Others 3
Goals: League 66, FA Cup 6, Europe 1, Others 2
Debut: League, 25 August 1951 v Arsenal (h) won 2–1

Also played for: Leyton Orient, Worcester City, Bromsgrove Rovers, Darlaston, England (2 caps)

Arsenal manager Tom Whittaker strode majestically into the Wolves dressing room on a sunny late afternoon in August 1951 to seek out 17-year-old Norman Deeley who, at the time, had been the smallest player ever to appear at senior level for the club. 'Well played young 'un' said Whittaker 'A fine debut... keep learning all the time and put a few inches on and you'll be alright.'

Deeley did just that. He kept learning and growing, rising from 4ft 11in on his debut to a maximum of 5ft 4in – but it was a worthwhile struggle right to the very top. He recalled 'Some folk thought that my height increased because Bert Williams and Billy Wright took my arms and legs each morning and gave me a jolly good tug. But it wasn't that simple. I conquered my lack of inches by hours of agonising body building exercises, but the real turning point came when manager Stan Cullis decided to switch me from being a right-half to a right-winger. I loved it.'

Amazingly, owing to the form of Johnny Hancocks, it took Deeley six years to establish himself in the Wolves first team. In fact, from his debut day in 1951 he made only 37 League appearances before making the outside-right position his own at the start of the 1957–58 season – which ended in glory as Wolves won the First Division title for the second time, Norman scoring 23 goals, second only to Jimmy Murray with 29.

The following season a second League Championship-winners' medal came Deeley's way after his brilliant displays on both flanks, which produced a further 17 League goals plus two in Cup action, and he was rewarded for his efforts with two England caps against the World Champions Brazil and Peru. He was now at the peak of his form, and he got even better in 1959–60 when Wolves won the FA Cup and finished runners-up in the League (behind Burnley). In the Cup Final at Wembley, he scored twice in a 3–0 win over Blackburn Rovers and as a result was voted Man of the Match, and deservedly so, for he teased and tormented the Rovers defence all afternoon in a rather scrappy contest. Earlier in that season he had netted four times in a 9–0 League win over Fulham under the Molineux floodlights, and afterwards the England skipper Johnny Haynes, who sat out the game through injury, said 'You were brilliant, Norm, absolutely brilliant.'

Deeley maintained his form throughout 1960–61 but then, as the team started to struggle, manager Cullis decided to change his wingers, introducing Terry Wharton on the right and Alan Hinton on the left. He also recruited Irish international Peter McParland as well as having Cliff Durandt available. Reluctantly Deeley moved on, joining Leyton Orient in February 1962 where he was later joined by his former Wolves colleague Bobby Mason. In the summer of 1964 he entered non-League football with Worcester City, and after spells with Bromsgrove Rovers and Darlaston he announced his retirement in 1974, aged 40. Residing in his native Wednesbury, he became manager of the Caldmore Community Centre in Walsall, and for many years he was the steward for the guest lounge at Fellows Park.

ROBBIE DENNISON

Date of birth: 30 April 1963, Banbridge, Northern Ireland

Wolves record:
Appearances: League 264+29, FA Cup 16+2, League Cup 12+4, Others 24+2
Goals: League 40, FA Cup 2, League Cup 3, Others 4
Debut: League, 14 March 1987 v Swansea City (h) won 4–0

Also played for: Glenavon, West Bromwich Albion, Swansea City (loan), Hednesford Town, Hereford United, Warley Borough, Warley Rangers, Northern Ireland (18 full, 3 B caps)

Wolves signed Robbie Dennison from neighbours West Bromwich Albion for what was to prove a bargain fee of just £20,000 in March 1987 – half of what Albion had paid for him from the Irish League club Glenavon in September 1985, and there's no doubt that he added purpose, skill and, more significantly, width to Graham Turner's side.

A positive player who loved to hug the touchline, Dennison occupied both flanks, preferring the left wing to the right. He enjoyed running at defenders, had a trick or two in both feet, centred the ball well and, when given the chance, could shoot with power and direction. He was also spot on with corner-kicks and quite often was given the chance to try his luck when a free-kick was awarded within shooting range of the goal posts.

Dennison followed striker Steve Bull and midfielder Andy Thompson to Molineux from The Hawthorns and was later joined by another ex-Baggies star, Ally Robertson. All four quickly bedded in together, and Dennison became a vital member of the team. In fact, being a winger, his and Bull's names were invariably first and second on the team sheet on a match day – so dependent was Turner on both players.

He played his part in helping Wolves win the Fourth Division Championship and Sherpa Van Trophy in his first full season at the club (1987–88), playing in 43 League games and 58 overall. The following season he missed only five competitive matches, scored 10 goals and again played a massive part in helping Wolves clinch promotion for the second year running as winners of the Third Division.

Around this time, Dennison was on fire. He was extremely confident before, during and after a match, and, above all, he was enjoying his football to the full. He was also a valuable member of the Northern Ireland squad, having won the first of his 18 full caps against France in Belfast in April 1987 (0–0). The remainder of his caps were won over the next 10 years, his last coming in 1997 as a substitute against Italy.

An ever present for the first time in his career in 1989–90 and still a regular the following season, Dennison continued to supply the crosses for Bull and Andy Mutch, but in 1991–92 he suffered a leg injury which knocked him back a stride or two. He regained full fitness, had a decent enough 1993–94 campaign but thereafter had to be at his best following the arrival of new boss Graham Taylor, who came with new ideas. He stuck in there, as always, and was in and out of the team over the next three years before moving to Hednesford Town in 1997 after a spell on loan with Swansea City. Rewarded with a testimonial after 11 years with Wolves, he later rejoined his former manager Graham Turner at Hereford before leaving football in 2002 to concentrate on his sports trophy business.

DICKY DORSETT

Date of birth: 3 December 1919, Brownhills, Staffordshire
Died: 1998, Brownhills, Staffordshire

Wolves record:
Appearances: League 46, FA Cup 6, Wartime 58
Goals: League 32, FA Cup 3, Wartime 40
Debut: League, 26 March 1938 v Charlton Athletic (a) lost 4–1

Also played for: Aston Villa and as a guest for Brentford, Grimsby Town, Liverpool, Queen's Park Rangers and Southampton during World War Two

Known as the 'Iron man' and also the 'Brownhills Bomber', Dicky Dorsett was as tough as they come, a rock-solid footballer, as strong as an ox and a player who never shirked a tackle. He shoulder-charged his opponents with aggressiveness and total commitment, was rugged to the last and, above all, his general outfield play was exceptional.

Signed by Wolves as a 15-year-old amateur in 1935, having been spotted playing (and scoring goals) for Walsall Boys and the Birmingham County FA, Dorsett turned professional in December 1936 and went on to spend the next 10 years at Molineux, although seven were lost due to the war, during which time he assisted five other League clubs up and down the country.

The fans loved tough guy Dicky who, in his early days, played in both the right-half and outside-left positions before settling down at inside-left as partner to Teddy Maguire.

In his first season as a professional at Molineux (1936–37), Dorsett acted as reserve to Tom Smalley and Bryn Jones, and it was the former he eventually replaced at right-half before switching to the left wing when, completely out of the blue, he slammed home four goals in an emphatic 10–1 home League win over Leicester City in April 1938 – this being only his fourth senior outing. He netted twice more at the end of that season and in 1938–39 claimed a further 29 goals as Wolves finished runners-up in both the League and FA Cup competitions. Having been moved inside, he missed only seven League games and played in all six Cup ties, having the pleasure (albeit to no avail) of scoring Wolves' only goal in the Final, which they lost 4–1 to Portsmouth.

After his wartime exploits, during which time he helped Wolves win the League North Cup (1942), Dorsett toured Denmark with his club in May–June 1946, and during a game in Copenhagen he was sent off for the first time in his career. 'It was harsh' he said. 'One of their players kicked me in the back as I was shielding the ball...so I told him precisely what I thought. He retorted by spitting at me, so I smacked him one in the face.' This incident upset the club (and his manager, Major Buckley), and as a result Dorsett never played for Wolves again and was transferred to Aston Villa for £3,000 in September 1946.

In January 1950 Dorsett's playing days almost came to an abrupt end when he was involved in a serious car crash. Thankfully he survived and went on to score 36 goals in 271 games for Villa before retiring in 1953 when he became youth- team coach. He was later assistant trainer at Liverpool and also managed Brownhills Boys' Club while employed by BRD & BIP (Strelly Works).

Dicky was the nephew of the former West Bromwich Albion and Manchester City brothers George and Joe Dorsett, who both played during the early years of the 20th century.

DEREK DOUGAN

Date of birth: 20 January 1938, Belfast, Northern Ireland

Wolves record:
Appearances: League 244+14, FA Cup 12, League Cup 22, Europe 18, Others 11+2
Goals: League 95, FA Cup 4, League Cup 7, Europe 12, Others 5
Debut: League, 18 March 1967 v Plymouth Argyle (a) won 1–0

Also played for: Distillery, Portsmouth, Blackburn Rovers, Peterborough United, Aston Villa, Leicester City, Northern Ireland (43 full and 2 B caps)
Managed: Kettering Town

One of the most colourful and controversial figures in soccer, Derek Dougan became the idol of the terraces when he joined Wolves for £50,000 from Leicester City in March 1967. His cause was greatly assisted when he netted a hat-trick on his home debut against Hull City – a game featured that evening on BBC's *Match of the Day*.

However, when Dougan returned to the club as chief executive under the notorious reign of the Bhatti brothers in 1982, the fortunes of Wolves spiralled out of control, and he appeared to lose favour with the supporters and, indeed, the local community.

Dougan played for Distillery before joining Portsmouth for £25,000 in August 1957, having already gained international caps at Schoolboy, Youth and Amateur levels as a wing-half and central-defender. Successfully converted into a striker at Fratton Park, over the next 18 years he scored 262 goals in 692 competitive games, including 222 in 546 League games – the most by an Irishman in English football.

Nicknamed 'the Doog', he was transferred to Blackburn Rovers in March 1959 and a little over a year later played in the FA Cup Final against Wolves, despite handing in a transfer request on the morning of the match. He eventually left Ewood Park for Aston Villa in a £15,000 deal in August 1961. Two years later he switched to Peterborough United and in May 1965 joined Leicester City. He spent two years at Filbert Street before manager Ronnie Allen greatly improved Wolves' promotion challenge by bringing him to Molineux. He netted nine goals in 11 games at the end of that 1966–67 campaign to help Wolves clinch promotion to the First Division along with Coventry City.

For the first two seasons in the top flight Dougan was top scorer with totals of 17 and 14 goals respectively, but his most prolific campaign came in 1971–72 when, joined in the attack by John Richards, he finished up with 24 goals, 12 coming in the UEFA Cup, the most ever by a Wolves player in European competition. He added three more to his tally later on as his partnership with Richards became one of the most feared in the country.

Wolves were agonisingly close to glory on several occasions in the early 1970s. Their only successes, and the only rewards for Dougan during his eight-year stay at Molineux, came in the Finals of the 1971 Texaco Cup and 1974 League Cup. He announced his retirement as a player at the end of the 1974–75 season, having donned the gold and black for the last time at senior level as a substitute against Leeds United at Molineux in front of 34,000 fans, who rose as one to bid their hero farewell.

Dougan's record of 123 goals in 323 first-class matches for Wolves included hat-tricks in the Football League, League Cup and UEFA Cup, and he netted twice against Arsenal in the 1973 FA Cup third-place Play-off match. He also hit eight goals in 43 full internationals for Northern Ireland between 1958 and 1973. Awarded a testimonial in the October of that year, he went on to have a spell as manager of non-League Kettering Town and was PFA chairman before his ill-fated return to Molineux.

Deeply involved in a fundraising scheme for the Duncan Edwards Medical Centre (Dudley) as well as being the author of several books, he now lives in Codsall.

JIMMY DUNN

Date of birth: 25 November 1923, Edinburgh

Wolves record:
Appearances: League 123, 7 FA Cup, Other 1, Wartime 100
Goals: League 33, FA Cup 0, Other 0, Wartime 15
Debut: League (North), 31 October 1942 v Crewe Alexandra (h) won 3–2

Also played for: Derby County, Worcester City, Runcorn.

The son of Jimmy Dunn, who starred in Scotland's brilliant Wembley Wizards team that whipped England 5–1 in 1928, Jimmy Dunn junior was certainly not as good as his father, but he was still a pretty decent footballer whose early career, like that of so many others, was considerably disrupted by World War Two.

Brought up in Liverpool, Dunn joined Wolves as an amateur in 1941 and signed a full professional contract in November 1942, despite being placed on standby to serve his country in France. He made exactly 100 appearances in regional competitions, scoring 15 goals, which put him in good stead for the recommencement of League football in August 1946. Owing to the form of inside-forwards Jesse Pye, Fred Ramscar and Willie Forbes, who all played either side of Dennis Westcott, unfortunately he had to bide his time in the reserves. In fact, he made only three senior appearances that season, scoring in the last against the League champions Liverpool at Molineux, which was also Stan Cullis's final outing as a Wolves player.

The following season, owing to injuries and occasional loss of form of other players, Jimmy became more of a regular, appearing in 28 first-class matches while occupying three different positions. He claimed nine goals, four in successive matches in April, including one against his future club Derby County. Named in the side at inside-right for the start of the 1948–49 campaign, he was switched to the inside-left berth halfway through proceedings, and he retained that spot with some splendid performances, two of his best coming in early FA Cup victories over Sheffield United at Bramall Lane and Liverpool at Molineux when he scored in each game. Wolves went on to reach the Final against Leicester City, and with Jimmy pulling the strings in centre-field they beat the Second Division battlers 3–1 to win the trophy for the third time.

A serious back injury affected Dunn's game in 1949–50 when he managed only eight appearances, but he was back to his best the following season (playing in a total of 39 games), and it was much of the same in 1951–52 when he made 26 starts. However, with Peter Broadbent now in the side and with manager Cullis planning for the future, he became surplus to requirements. He was subsequently transferred to struggling Derby County, who considered him to be the experienced player that might help them avoid relegation. Only six weeks after joining the Rams he was forced out with a cartilage injury that required surgery. He came back but Derby still went down, and in 1955 Dunn left the Baseball Ground for Worcester City, later assisting Runcorn before returning to Wolverhampton to take over the Roebuck pub in Penn.

In the mid 1960s he was appointed coach by West Bromwich Albion and twice went to Wembley with the Baggies (losing in the League Cup Final of 1967 but winning the FA Cup a year later). A qualified physiotherapist, Jimmy worked for the Edgbaston Clinic (Birmingham) after leaving The Hawthorns and was employed as a rep in Dudley while running his own gymnasium in the jewellery quarter of Birmingham.

Now living in retirement in Cradley Heath, he played tennis at the Quinton Tennis Club until well into his 70s.

GEORGE EDMONDS

Date of birth:	4 April 1893, Holborn, London
Died:	10 December 1989, Ryde, Isle of Wight

Wolves record:

Appearances:	League 115, FA Cup 11
Goals:	League 38, FA Cup 4
Debut:	League, 28 August 1920 v Fulham (a) lost 2–0
Also played for:	St Stephen's FC, Andrew's FC, St Albans City, Watford, Fulham, Northfleet

George Edmonds spent much of his early life living in the St Albans area, and after two excellent seasons with his local club he joined Watford as a professional in 1912. An out-and-out striker, he scored 18 goals in 35 appearances for the Hornets when they won the Southern League Championship in 1915 and weighed in with another 20 for the same club when they finished runners-up in the first season after World War One.

Hugely impressed with Edmonds's marksmanship, Wolves, who were desperately in need of a robust, direct and established centre-forward – having used no fewer than 10 different players in that position the previous season – eventually acquired his services for just £150 early in August 1920 – just in time for the new season. He made an immediate impact by netting 15 goals in 45 games as Wolves managed to escape relegation by three points and reached the FA Cup Final. Unfortunately he was not as his best on a muddy Stamford Bridge pitch, and as a result a much fitter and stronger Spurs team collected the trophy with a 1–0 victory.

Well built, quick over 15–20 yards, with a powerful right-foot shot, Edmonds was an aggressive footballer, extremely dangerous in the air and a player who knew no fear whatsoever. Indeed, he was regularly treated for cuts to the head, once receiving 10 stitches above his right eye.

After having a variety of different attacking partners over a period of two seasons, Edmonds finally settled down to form a splendid strike duo with the former Everton forward Stan Fazackerley. The pair shared 27 goals in 1922–23, George claiming his first hat-trick for Wolves in a 3–0 home League win over Port Vale in April 1923. Their efforts, however, were all in vain as Wolves suffered relegation to the Third Division North for the first time in their history.

Bitterly disappointed, Edmonds asked to leave Molineux and his wish was granted, Wolves selling him to Fulham for £250. He failed to get into the Cottagers first XI due to niggling knee and ankle injuries, and in 1926 he returned to Watford and entered non-League football with Northfleet soon afterwards, before announcing his retirement in May 1929.

The scorer of 120 goals in 288 Football and Southern League appearances, Edmonds continued to watch football right up until his late 70s. He spent his last years in a nursing home in Ryde on the Isle of Wight, passing away in December 1989 at the ripe old age of 96.

In the home League game against Bristol City in September 1920, a shot from George went straight through the net. The referee, however, disallowed the 'goal' and the game finished level at 0–0.

umbro

MEL EVES

Date of birth:	19 September 1956, Wednesbury

Wolves record:

Appearances:	League 169+11, FA Cup 19, League Cup 12+1, Europe 2
Goals:	League 44, FA Cup 5, League Cup 3, Europe 1
Debut:	League, 26 November 1977 v Ipswich Town (h) drew 0–0
Also played for:	Huddersfield Town, Sheffield United, Gillingham, Mansfield Town, West Bromwich Albion (reserves), Telford United, Cheltenham Town, Old Wulfrunians, England (3 B caps)
Managed:	Willenhall Town

Mel Eves spent 11 years at Molineux. In that time he scored 53 goals in 214 senior games, helping Wolves win the League Cup in 1980 – the proudest and happiest moment of his career. He joined the club as an apprentice in July 1973 and turned professional two years later. However, with John Richards, Bobby Gould and Steve Kindon and then Norman Bell and Alan Sunderland all ahead of him when it came to team selection, he spent two seasons in the reserves, netting plenty of goals while gaining valuable experience when competing against senior professionals.

Eves finally made the breakthrough four months into the 1977–78 season when manager Sammy Chung gave him his League debut against Ipswich Town, joining Richards to form the main strike force in the absence of Bell. After a run of four games, including a visit to Old Trafford when almost 49,000 fans saw Wolves lose 3–1, he had to wait until mid-January for his fifth outing. He ended the campaign with 12 appearances under his belt and three goals scored, the first earning a point from a 1–1 draw at Chelsea. The following season, during which John Barnwell took over as manager, he made 22 appearances, including his first in the FA Cup at Brighton.

For the 1979–80 campaign Scottish international Andy Gray was signed to boost the Wolves attack, and at that point Eves, a good, honest footballer with plenty of skill, pace and shooting power, looked set to return to the reserves. But Barnwell elected to play him on the left with Gray and Richards through the middle, and as a result he had his best run in the first team, appearing in 40 matches, and celebrated in March with a League Cup-winners' prize after Wolves beat Nottingham Forest 1–0 at Wembley. Winning that trophy earned Wolves a place in the UEFA Cup, and Eves scored in the first-round home leg over PSV Eindhoven, but it was to no avail as the Dutch side won 3–2 on aggregate.

Unfortunately, in the League Wolves struggled despite Richards, Gray and Eves scoring 27 goals between them. Things got worse the following season, and, although Eves had the pleasure of being leading marksman, Wolves were relegated to the Second Division. With Wayne Clarke then joining him and Gray up front (in place of Richards), he again headed the scoring charts in 1982–83 when promotion was gained at the first attempt, Wolves taking second spot behind the champions QPR.

As Gray departed, several fresh faces came into the side, many of them accompanying Eves in the forward line. But once again Wolves had a terrible time, finishing bottom of the table after winning only six League games.

In December 1984, following a loan spell at Huddersfield, Tommy Docherty – the sixth manager at Molineux in 10 years – sold Eves to Sheffield United, where he spent two years before transferring to Gillingham. After loan spells with Manchester City, Mansfield Town and West Bromwich Albion, he quit competitive football in 1989 with an impressive record of 69 goals in 273 games. He also played three times for England's B team versus Singapore (twice) and New Zealand in June 1978.

Eves assisted Telford United and Cheltenham Town in the Vauxhall Conference and also played for the Old Wulfrunians before becoming a football agent in the late 1990s, and then entering management for the first time in March 2006 with Willenhall Town, naming ex-Wolves player Dean Edwards as his assistant.

TED FARMER

Date of birth: 21 January 1940, Rowley Regis, Staffordshire

Wolves record:
Appearances: League 57, FA Cup 2, Europe 3
Goals: League 44, FA Cup 0, Europe 0
Debut: League, 24 September 1960 v Manchester United (a) won 3–1

Also played for: Wednesbury Commercial, Wednesbury Youth Club, England (2 Under-23 caps)

Unfortunately Ted Farmer played only four seasons of League football before injury forced him to retire at the age of 24. As a youngster he was a prolific marksman for Wednesbury High School, Rowley Regis Boys and Dudley & District Schools, once netting 11 goals in one game and nine in another. Building up his strength by playing at weekends for the Wednesbury Commercial and Wednesbury Youth clubs, he often starred in two games a day and sometimes three in 48 hours. In fact, on a cold, dank Saturday in November 1955 he scored 21 goals – 13 in the morning, eight in the afternoon.

Wolves, who had been monitoring Farmer's progress, gave him a trial in the summer of 1956. Impressing all and sundry, he was signed as an amateur, and in his first season in the old gold and black strip he rattled in 86 goals for the junior side. Manager Stan Cullis was mightily impressed, and after a positive run in the reserves Farmer was handed his First Division debut against Manchester United at Old Trafford in September 1960. Taking over from Jimmy Murray, he celebrated in style by scoring twice in a 3–1 win before 44,458 spectators.

Farmer had a wonderful 1960–61 season. Between them he and Murray netted 53 goals, Ted finishing up as leading marksman with a total of 28, which included a sparkling hat-trick in a 5–3 home win over Arsenal and a four-timer when Birmingham City were blasted 5–1, also at Molineux. One spell realised 11 goals in six games and only an injury that laid him low for the last five matches prevented him from becoming the first Wolves player to net 30 League goals in a season since Dennis Westcott in 1946–47.

In November 1961 Farmer was capped twice by England at Under-23 level, scoring once in a 7–1 win over Israel at Leeds and firing home a hat-trick in a 5–2 victory over Holland in Rotterdam, Bobby Moore having a hand in two of his goals. Shortly after coming back from Holland, he was badly hurt at Fulham. Five weeks later that same injury was diagnosed as a broken leg! He was out for over four months and made only 11 appearances that season.

When on song and fully fit, Farmer proved to be a strong, brave, confident and exciting footballer. Possessing good pace over 20 to 30 yards, he preferred to use his right foot, and when he did let fly invariably he made the goalkeeper work. He was never afraid to shoot from any distance, and he was also a pretty useful header of the ball as well.

Injuries seriously affected Farmer's game in 1962–63 when he managed only 13 senior appearances, scoring nine goals, four coming in an opening day 8–1 demolition job on Manchester City followed by two in his next game versus West Ham. The following year he struggled once more, playing only six times, and with his right knee causing him pain he simply couldn't carry on, so he announced his retirement in 1964. So, once again, injury had robbed Wolves of another tremendous goalscoring centre-forward. Roy Swinbourne had been forced to retire in 1957 before he was 28.

Farmer had gone through hell in four years and only he, his close friends and, of course, the trainers and his manager at Molineux knew the extent of his injuries, of which he had many, including a damaged bladder, broken leg, numerous dislocations, a couple of bad twists, a handful of cracked ribs, a few chipped bones, concussion (twice) plus the familiar sprains and strains...even boxers don't suffer this sort of torture.

In the later 1960s Ted became licensee of the Lamp Tavern, Dudley, and in 1986 he published a book about his short career. When he quit it was a sad loss for the game.

MALCOLM FINLAYSON

Date of birth: 14 June 1930, Alexandria, Dunbartonshire, Scotland

Wolves record:
Appearances: League 179, FA Cup 14, Europe 8, Others 2
Goals: 0
Debut: League, 15 September 1956 v Leeds United (h) lost 2–1

Also played for: Renfrew Juniors, Millwall

Signed as cover for England international goalkeeper Bert Williams in readiness for the 1956–57 season, Malcolm Finlayson, then aged 26, was already a very experienced professional, having appeared in 251 competitive games for Millwall. He joined the London club in February 1948 from the Scottish intermediate club Renfrew Juniors after excelling in a hastily arranged 'behind-closed-doors' trial match at The Den. In fact, he was only 17 when he made his senior debut for the Lions, which came just 16 days after his trial.

At 6ft 1in tall and weighing 13 stone, Finlayson was ideally built for a goalkeeper and became one of the best produced by Millwall, for whom he would have played in many more games but for his national service in the Army. Agile with a safe pair of hands and sound positioning, he was also courageous and commanded his area well. He was a great favourite with the Lions supporters. In one game, against Walsall, he was taken to hospital in the 20th minute with his side losing 3–1, but, after being examined and stitched up, he returned to the ground, scaled the perimeter wall and re-entered the action 18 minutes into the second half, inspiring Millwall to a 6–5 victory.

It was much of the same at Molineux – once Finlayson had established himself in the first team. His bravery was never questioned and many times he kept Wolves in the match with some outstanding saves, often flinging himself at the feet of an opponent to avert danger. He had 13 outings in his first season with Wolves before taking over from Williams at the start of the 1957–58 campaign, which ended with him receiving a League Championship-winners' medal. He then collected a second winners' prize in the same competition 12 months later, and in 1960 he was jubilant as he played his part in Wolves' 3–0 FA Cup Final victory over Blackburn Rovers.

Retaining his place in the first team for the next two campaigns (injuries apart), Finlayson was then challenged for the number-one position by Fred Davies, who eventually took over between the posts in 1962. Over a period of five years – from August 1957 to May 1962 – Wolves participated in 210 League games. He appeared in 164 of them, a measure of his consistency, and when fit he was always first choice in the eyes of his manager Stan Cullis.

After spending two years in the reserves, Finlayson – whose last game for Wolves was at Anfield in September 1963 when he broke his finger – announced his retirement in May 1964 after eight seasons at Molineux, during which time he appeared in more than 200 senior games. For the record, a lot of people were surprised that he never received international recognition of any sort....especially when you consider the goalkeeping dilemma that faced Scotland during the 1950s and early '60s! Later in life he became a director of R & F Stockholders of Kingswinford near Dudley, and in June 1982, following the resignation of chairman Harry Marshall and other members of the board, he took over as vice-chairman of Wolves, but this appointment lasted only a short while as he left the club when the Bhatti brothers took over. He still follows Wolves' fortunes to this day, mainly from his armchair rather than from a seat in the stand at Molineux.

ALBERT FLETCHER

Date of birth:	4 June 1867, Wolverhampton
Died:	1938, Wolverhampton

Wolves record:

Appearances:	League 59, FA Cup 17
Goals:	League 1, FA Cup 1
Debut:	FA Cup, 15 October 1887 v Walsall Town (a) won 2–1
Also played for:	Willenhall Pickwick

Albert Fletcher was 19 years of age when he joined Wolves from the local team Willenhall Pickwick in the summer of 1886, a golden sovereign securing his transfer in secretary-manager Jack Addenbrooke's office. However, with Arthur Lowder seemingly secure in the right-half position, alongside Harry Allen and Alf Pearson in Wolves' middle line, he had to wait a year before making his senior debut, eventually starring in a first-round FA Cup win over Walsall Town at Dudley Road. From that day on he was a permanent fixture in the side, often producing some brilliant performances in defence and also in the centre of the field. He played in Wolves' first-ever Football League match against Aston Villa on 8 September 1888, scored his first goal for the club in a thrilling 4–4 draw away to Accrington a month later and at the end of that season collected a runners'-up medal after Preston North End (the firm favourites) had beaten Wolves 3–0 in the FA Cup Final at The Oval.

Fletcher made 22 appearances that season and his form was duly recognised by the England selectors, who awarded him with the first of his two full caps against Wales at the Victoria Ground, Stoke, when he lined up alongside his clubmate Arthur Lowder in a 4–1 win. A year later he played in his second international, also against Wales, this time at Wrexham, and finished up on the winning side once more by 3–1.

Well built with broad shoulders, Fletcher brought those physical advantages to bear when carrying out his wing-half duties. He was a hard worker, strong in the tackle, quick in recovery, and although he marred his performances at times with some reckless challenges he was, nonetheless, a terrific all-round footballer who encouraged the younger players around him.

Unfortunately a broken leg mishap – suffered during a 6–0 defeat by Aston Villa in a Birmingham Senior Cup tie at Perry Barr in March 1891, just a week after Wolves had lost 1–0 to Blackburn Rovers in the FA Cup semi-final – forced Fletcher to retire prematurely at the age of 24, this after he had made 76 first-class appearances for the Wanderers (124 if you include all local competitions). He was immediately appointed assistant trainer to Jack Lewis, a position he held for five years, at which point (May 1896) he was upgraded to head trainer at Molineux. He went on to serve the club in that capacity for the next 24 years, finally calling it a day at the end of the 1919–20 season, although he was asked to attend the 1921 FA Cup Final as assistant to Elijah Morse, ironically a game Wolves lost 1–0 to Morse's former club Tottenham Hotspur at Stamford Bridge.

Prior to that the well-respected Fletcher was 'sponge man' at the 1908 Final when Newcastle were defeated 3–1 at Crystal Palace, and occasionally he was placed on standby to look after the England team for certain internationals that were scheduled to take place in the Midlands.

Albert, who continued to visit Molineux as often as he could, remained in his native Wolverhampton until his death in 1938.

RON FLOWERS

Date of birth: 28 July 1934, Edlington near Doncaster, South Yorkshire

Wolves record:
Appearances: League 467, FA Cup 34, Europe 11, Others 3
Goals: League 33, FA Cup 4, Europe 0, Others 0
Debut: League, 20 September 1952 v Blackpool (h) lost 5–2

Also played for: Wath Wanderers, Northampton Town, Wellington Town, England (49 full, 2 Under-23 caps)
Managed: Wellington Town

A Yorkshireman, who developed through the junior ranks at Molineux, initially playing for the club's junior side Wath Wanderers, Ron Flowers was a big, strong, industrious wing-half who preferred the attacking game where he could indulge his hard shooting with both feet. Tenacious in the tackle and enormous in stamina, like his distinguished blond hair he stood head and shoulders above his opponents on many occasions as he powered his way forward from centre field, making a major contribution to Wolves' success during the 1950s.

After a rather subdued debut when Wolves were taken apart by a fine Blackpool side at Molineux in front of almost 49,000 spectators in 1952, Stanley Matthews having a field day, Flowers put that disappointment behind him, and the following season (1953–54) he made 15 appearances as Wolves won the League title for the first time in the club's history. He linked up superbly with Peter Broadbent in the engine room and was a fine passer of the ball, often bringing his wingers into play with sweeping passes to both flanks. He gave Wolves excellent service for 15 years, playing in over 500 senior games, making him the fifth-highest in the club's appearance records. In the space of six seasons he won three League Championship medals (adding triumphs in 1958 and 1959 to his success in 1954) and was a member of Wolves' FA Cup-winning side in 1960.

Part of a terrific middle line comprising, initially, himself, Bill Shorthouse and Billy Wright, then with Eddie Clamp and Wright and latterly with Clamp and Bill Slater, Flowers actually caused some anxiety in 1960 when he refused to re-sign for the club, but his differences were soon sorted out, obviously for the better! Between 1955 and 1966 he scored 10 goals (six from the penalty spot) in 49 internationals for England, captaining the side three times. He appeared in the 1962 World Cup Finals and was a member of Alf Ramsey's squad in 1966. His international debut was against France in Paris and his last outing was against Norway in Oslo a month before England's World Cup triumph. He was outstanding in an 8–1 win over the USA in Los Angeles in May 1959 and played even better when Scotland were battered 9–3 at Wembley two years later, having a hand in five of England's goals. But that's what he did best – creating chances for his colleagues. He also won two Under-23 caps, made 13 appearances for the Football League and played in seven other representative games.

Flowers stayed at Molineux just long enough to see Wolves regain their First Division status after relegation in 1965 before leaving to join Northampton Town in September 1967, later taking over as player-coach of the Cobblers prior to having a decent spell as player-manager of Wellington Town. When he returned to Molineux for a belated testimonial match in 1970–71, over 21,000 fans saw Wolves beat an England XI 8–4.

Ron, whose father and brother both played for Doncaster Rovers, ran a sports-outfitters shop in Wolverhampton for several years after quitting the football scene.

TOM GALLEY

Date of birth:	4 August 1915, Hednesford, Staffordshire
Died:	2000, Cannock

Wolves record:

Appearances:	League 183, FA Cup 21, Wartime 74
Goals:	League 41, FA Cup 8, Wartime 8
Debut:	League, 5 January 1935 v Sunderland (a) drew 0–0
Also played for:	Cannock Town, Notts County (amateur), Grimsby Town, Kidderminster Harriers, Clacton Town, England (2 caps)

Tom Galley was a real all-round footballer who could occupy the right-half and inside-right positions, chiefly, centre-half, but left-half and centre-forward on other occasions. Tall and rangy in build, he had ball command and an attacking flair and proved to be a loyal and dedicated club man who served Wolves for well over 13 years, during which time he appeared in almost 280 first-team matches (74 during wartime), doing so without complaint regardless of the position he was asked to play in.

After developing his football locally and having a brief spell as an amateur with Notts County, Galley joined Wolves as a part-time player in August 1933, signing a full contract in April 1934. At the time he was an out-and-out centre-forward, and after some excellent performances for the reserves he made his League debut at Sunderland halfway through the 1934–35 season, replacing the injured David 'Boy' Martin as leader of the attack. Martin had established himself in the side and with fellow strikers Billy Hartill, Bob Iverson and Gordon Clayton also at the club, and seemingly ahead of Tom in the selection stakes, he bided his time in the second XI before gaining a regular place in the first team during the second half of the 1935–36 campaign when he was switched to the wing-half position, playing on both flanks.

Now regarded as a versatile footballer, Galley had his best season at Molineux in 1936–37 when, occupying three different positions, he missed only six League games and one FA Cup tie, scoring 16 goals, all from the inside-right berth when he formed a wonderful partnership up front with Clayton. His height was a great asset, and he used this to perfection when heading towards goal or knocking down centres for his colleagues. He was not the fastest of players over the ground, but his form had improved immensely, and on 14 May 1937 he won his first full England cap, scoring in a 6–0 win over Norway in Oslo. He played in his second international 72 hours later, in a 4–0 win over Sweden in Stockholm and later, in 1938, he represented the Football League against the Scottish League.

Back to the bread and butter of League football, Galley had now been joined in the forward line by Dennis Westcott, who arrived at Molineux in February 1937. They scored 33 goals between them in 1937–38 when Wolves finished runners-up in the First Division, and the same duo followed on with another 55 in 1938–39 (Tom being an ever present) as Wolves once more had to settle for second spot in the League table as well as claiming the runners'-up prize in the FA Cup Final when they were defeated 4–1 by Portsmouth.

During the war Galley served in France and Germany with the Royal Artillery and guested for Aldershot, Clapton Orient, Leeds United and Watford and helped Wolves win the League North Cup in 1942. After the hostilities he added a further 45 senior appearances to his tally and scored his first hat-trick for Wolves in an 8–1 FA Cup win over Lovells Athletic in January 1946 before transferring north to Grimsby Town, whom he captained for a season before injuries caught up with him. He later assisted Kidderminster Harriers (1949–50) and then had a spell as player-coach of Clacton Town before returning home to manage a local team in Cannock, retiring from football in 1960.

Tom was also a very good club cricketer (he played this sport for 30 years) and his nephew, John Galley, played for Wolves in the 1960s as well as serving with Rotherham United, Bristol City, Nottingham Forest, Peterborough United and Hereford United.

JOE GARDINER

Date of birth: 23 August 1916, Bearpark, County Durham
Died: 1997, Sedgley near Wolverhampton

Wolves record:
Appearances: League 121, FA Cup 18, Wartime 49
Goals: League 2, FA Cup 0, Wartime 4
Debut: League, 23 February 1935 v West Bromwich Albion (a) lost 5–2

One of Major Frank Buckley's 'Molineux Babes', Joe Gardiner was only 18 years of age when he deputised for Dai Richards at left-half in Wolves' away League game against neighbours West Bromwich Albion in February 1935. It was a tough start as the Baggies won 5–2 in front of almost 32,000 fans.

Gardiner quickly put that defeat behind him, and when Richards joined Brentford nine months later he stepped forward again, joining Tom Galley and Bill Morris in the middle line. He held his place for two months and made 21 first-team appearances that season, scoring two goals, the first in an 8–1 home win over Blackburn and the second in a 2–0 victory at Liverpool. He followed up with 33 outings in 1936–37 when, most of the time, the regular half-back trio comprised Tom Smalley at right-half, Stan Cullis in the centre and Joe on the left.

Originally a bustling, black-haired centre-forward, Gardiner developed into a tough-tackling defender, well built with good stamina. He took no prisoners and was regarded as one of the most reliable and committed wing-halves in the First Division. Never one to shy away from a challenge, he battled on regardless and covered acres of ground every game he played in. A real down-to-earth defender with a heart of gold, he was one of Wolves' unsung heroes over a period of four years leading up to World War Two.

Gardiner missed only four games in 1937–38 when Wolves finished runners-up in Division One and played in the same number of matches the following season when second spot was claimed again. He was also a member of Wolves' FA Cup Final side in 1939, but, along with his 10 teammates, he walked off the Wembley pitch with a rather forlorn look on his face after Portsmouth had upset the applecart by winning 4–1.

Gardiner, who played on through the war, making almost 50 appearances in regional competitions, eventually retired in May 1944. Remaining on the club's training staff, he became a great friend of Stan Cullis. They worked tremendously well together, and Stan even recommended that Joe should act as trainer to the England team, which he did when Wales visited Villa Park in 1958.

Gardiner made over 180 first-team appearances for Wolves (including wartime), and although he didn't gain a winners' medal of any kind during his time as a player at Molineux (but did represent the Football League against the Scottish League on his home patch as a 22-year-old) he certainly made amends as a trainer, collecting awards when the team won the FA Cup in 1949 and 1960 and clinched the League Championship in 1954, 1958 and 1959, and there haven't been too many sponge-men who can match that sort of record!

Born in the same village as the former Derby County and England player Sammy Crooks, he represented Durham County Boys as a teenager before joining Wolves as an amateur in December 1932, turning professional nine months later. He spent over two and a half seasons playing Central League football before entering the big time in 1935.

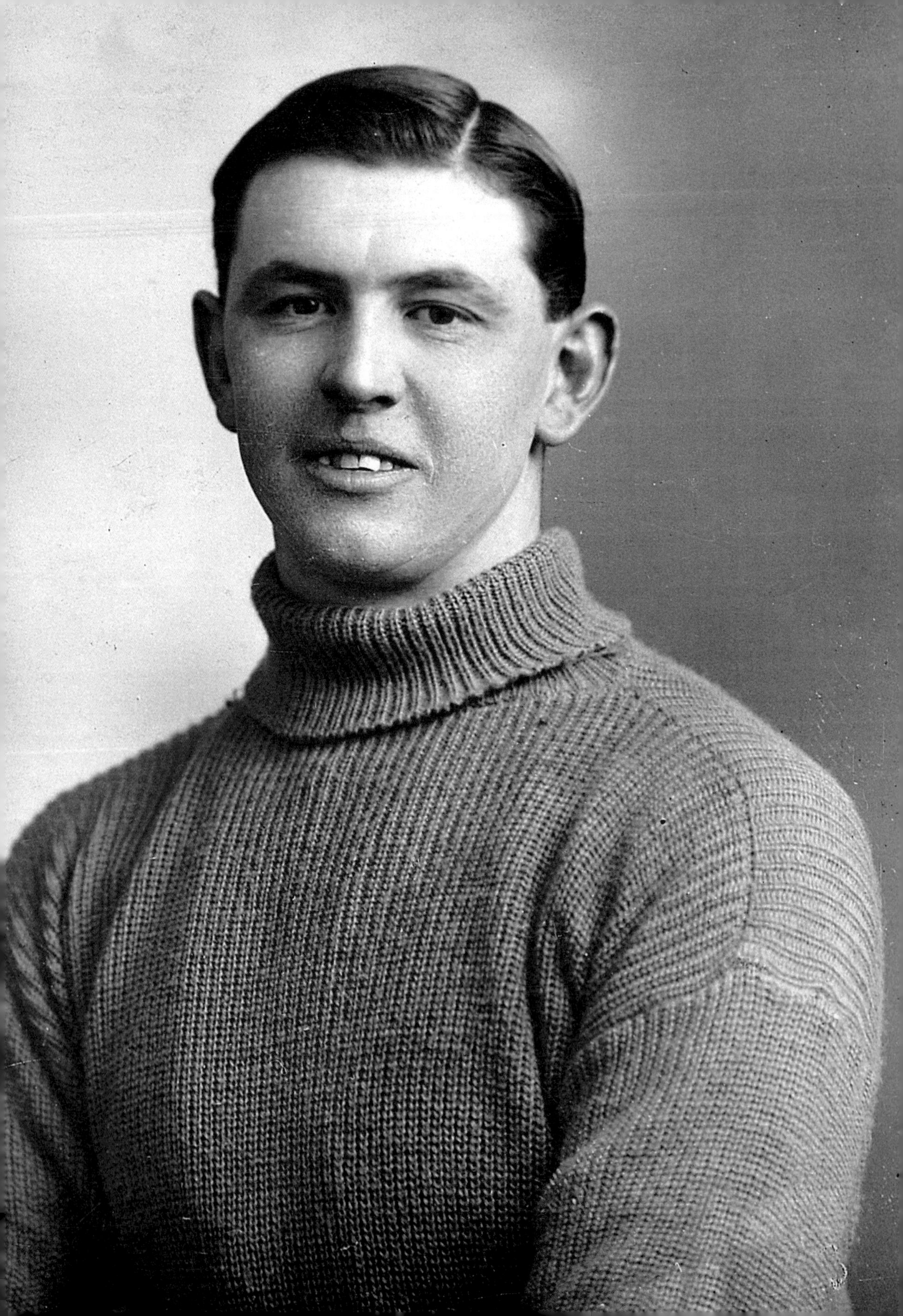

NOEL GEORGE

Date of birth: 26 December 1897, Lichfield
Died: 16 October 1929, Lichfield

Wolves record:
Appearances: League 222, FA Cup 20
Goals: 0
Debut: FA Cup, 3 February 1921 v Derby County (h) won 1–0

Also played for: Hednesford Town

In a newspaper write-up in 1923, goalkeeper Noel George was described as being 'Cool, confident, reliable and modest in character, who made hard shots look easy.' Not the tallest of 'keepers, he was also agile, a safe handler of the ball, confident on his line and brave, often choosing to dive at the feet of his opponent to prevent a goal from being scored or a chance being set up.

When serving with the Royal Artillery Second Command in Greece during the Great War, George was asked, in an emergency, to play in goal for his unit. He did okay, and although not too keen he continued between the posts and improved as time passed by; so much so, that in April 1919 he was chosen to keep goal for a Salonika Select XI against an Italian XI at Aldershot in a challenge match to celebrate the end of the hostilities. He played a blinder and never looked back after that.

Originally a centre-forward with his local team in Lichfield, George also played for Hednesford Town in the same position before enlisting in the Army. In July 1919, after officially being demobbed, he was asked to join Wolves – as a goalkeeper – and within 18 months had established himself in the club's League side, taking over the duties from Teddy Peers. He had made an impressive debut in a second-round FA Cup replay against Derby County on a cold, dank Thursday afternoon in February 1921 when almost 40,000 fans saw Wolves win 1–0. He kept his place and played in that season's Final against Tottenham Hotspur at Stamford Bridge when Wolves lost 1–0 in the Chelsea mud.

George was an ever present in 1921–22 when he conceded 49 goals in 42 League games, but he missed almost half of the fixtures the following season when Wolves were relegated from the Second Division. However, he was in top form throughout the 1923–24 campaign when the Third Division North title was won and promotion gained at the first attempt. He appeared in every game, let in only 27 goals (four scored by Wigan Borough) and kept 23 clean sheets, and he was ear-marked for a possible England call-up, which did not materialise when Bill Sewell of Blackburn (deputising for Huddersfield's Ted Taylor) declared himself fit before the international against Wales at Ewood Park in the March. Admittedly he had a strong defence in front of him – Ted Watson, Harold Shaw, George Getgood, Bill Caddick and Albert Kay – but he still performed superbly well and even saved two vital penalties.

George continued to produce quality performances over the next two seasons, being an ever present for a third time in 1924–25. Around now, though, he started to struggle with injuries and missed several matches. He also complained of feeling unwell with head and neck pains, and although he managed to train and play at weekends he was not the same man.

Sadly, after a 4–0 League defeat at Bristol City in November 1927, when he was far from his best, George was admitted to a Wolverhampton hospital with a terminal illness. He bravely fought the illness for almost two years but eventually died peacefully in his sleep in a Lichfield infirmary just two months short of his 32nd birthday.

ANDY GRAY

Date of birth: 30 November 1955, Gorbals, Glasgow

Wolves record:
Appearances: League 130+3, FA Cup 13, League Cup 14, Europe 2
Goals: League 38, FA Cup 3, League Cup 3, Europe 1
Debut: League, 15 September 1979 v Everton (a) won 3–2

Also played for: Clydebank Strollers, Dundee United, Aston Villa (two spells), Everton, Notts County, West Bromwich Albion, Glasgow Rangers, Cheltenham Town, Scotland (4 Under-23 and 20 full caps)

Surprisingly Andy Gray supported Hibernian as a lad, but he also enjoyed watching Glasgow Rangers. Prior to leaving school, he was registered as an amateur with Dundee United, who rewarded him with a professional contract in May 1973. The scorer of 45 goals in 86 appearances north of the border, he gained a Scottish Cup runners'-up medal in 1974 before transferring to Aston Villa for £110,000 three years later. Spending just over two seasons with the Birmingham club, he helped Villa win the League Cup in 1977 while also being voted the PFA Player of the Year and Young Player of the Year.

In September 1979, after netting 69 times in 144 games for Villa, Gray became the most expensive footballer in Britain when Wolves manager John Barnwell paid £1.15m (£1.46 with the various extras added on) for his signature, the transfer being completed on the Molineux pitch before Wolves' home League game with Crystal Palace.

A colourful character in more ways than one, both on and off the field, Gray was a brave, strong and confident striker and a tremendous header of the ball who led the line with great determination. He was a never-say-die sort of player, totally committed to playing football. He was one of the great old-fashioned centre-forwards to emerge since World War Two, and he certainly made defenders earn their keep with his powerful and courageous displays inside the penalty area – which caused him several injuries, mainly to his head!

Taking over from Billy Rafferty, Gray made an impressive start to his Wolves career. Partnering John Richards in attack, he scored four goals in his first three outings, including a decisive one on his debut at Goodison Park, a game Wolves won 3–2. He ended his first season at Molineux with 15 goals to his credit, 12 in the League and three in Cup competitions, the last of these being a dramatic tap-in winner that decided the League Cup Final in Wolves' favour by a goal to nil over Nottingham Forest.

Confident in his own ability, Gray netted 11 times in 1980–81 but struggled with the rest of his colleagues the following season as Wolves were relegated to the Second Division. Obviously disappointed, he stuck to his task – that of scoring goals – and in 1982–83, with Mel Eves and Wayne Clarke assisting up front, he grabbed 10 in the League, including vital strikes against Derby County and Crystal Palace, as Wolves gained promotion at the first attempt, finishing runners-up to Queen's Park Rangers. By this time he was already an established Scottish international, having won his first full cap against Romania in December 1975 when registered with Aston Villa. He went on to play 20 times for his country's senior side (13 as a Wolves player) and scored six goals. He also represented Scotland at Youth-team level and in four Under-23 matches.

Back in the top flight of English football, and playing under a new manager (Graham Hawkins), Gray made only 10 appearances for Wolves during the first part of the 1983–84 campaign before transferring to Everton for £250,000, signed to replace Graeme Sharp. During his time at Goodison Park he gained winners' medals in three major competitions: the League Championship, FA Cup (scoring against Watford in the 1984 Final) and European Cup-winners' Cup (when he also found the net in the Final against Rapid Vienna). Villa re-signed him as a stop-gap in 1985 for £150,000, and after spells at Notts County (loan) and West Bromwich Albion (signed by his former boss Ron Saunders) he moved to Ibrox, helping Rangers win the Premier League and reach the League Cup Final in 1989. Job done, he then played briefly for Cheltenham Town before retiring in 1991, having amassed a career record in club and international football of 215 goals in 614 games.

Andy returned to Villa Park for a third time as assistant to manager Ron Atkinson before quitting active football in 1992 to concentrate on his role as analyst and pundit for soccer on Sky Sports.

VAL GREGORY

Date of birth: 14 February 1888, Hendon, Middlesex
Died: 10 March 1940, Heath Town, Wolverhampton

Wolves record:
Appearances: League 96, FA Cup 10
Goals: League 2, FA Cup 0
Debut: League, 28 August 1920 v Fulham (a) lost 2–0

Also played for: Reading, Watford, Arsenal

A note in a match-day programme described Val Gregory as being '...an exceptionally smart tackler, aggressive and perceptive, a purveyor of passes that could split the tightest defence.' There was certainly nothing untidy about his football – coolness personified at times – and he was a most serviceable, all-round player who, one feels, would have gone on to greater things if he'd been with a more 'fashionable' club.

Gregory joined Wolves at a time when things weren't going all that well out on the pitch. The team had finished a disappointing 19th in the Second Division in the first season after World War One, and manager Jack Addenbrooke desperately needed someone in authority in the middle of the park. Despite not having played in the Football League (all his previous experience had come at Southern League level), he fitted that bill to a tee, and following his £3,500 transfer from Arsenal he quickly slotted into the team at right-half in place of Alf Riley who was switched to the other flank, with Woodward occupying the central role.

Wolves' form improved greatly as Gregory, who took over the captaincy for a while, urged his players on with some gritty performances, especially in the FA Cup competition. In fact, they reached the Final after knocking out Stoke, Derby County, Fulham, Everton and Cardiff City, and with Val in fine form they were confident of beating Tottenham Hotspur at Stamford Bridge. But despite another courageous, battling performance by the Wolves right-half, it was Spurs who squeezed home, winning 1–0 on a muddy Chelsea pitch.

Wolves edged up to 15th in the table in 1920–21, Gregory missing 10 League games through injury and illness. The following season he was absent three times as the team slipped down the ladder to 17th after a horrible second half to the campaign when they won only three times in 20 starts. And it got even worse when, in 1922–23, for the first time in the club's history, they were relegated to the Third Division North. No blame could be put on Gregory. He again played his heart out but a lack of goals – only 42 scored in 42 games – was Wolves' downfall, and they fell from grace in last place, nine points from safety.

Gregory remained a registered player at Molineux until the summer of 1925 when he officially retired, taking over as coach and later assisting the club as a trainer. Ill-health caused him to call it a day in 1938, and two years later he died, aged 52. Born the son of a schoolteacher on St Valentine's Day (hence his name) Val, who was initially a centre-half, spent two seasons with Reading (from May 1908) and three with Watford before joining Arsenal in September 1914. He failed to make a single first-team appearance for the Gunners and had no hesitation in joining Wolves.

JOHNNY HANCOCKS

Date of birth:	30 April 1919, Oakengates, Shropshire
Died:	19 February, 1994, Oakengates, Shropshire

Wolves record:

Appearances:	League 343, FA Cup 33, Others 2
Goals:	League 158, FA Cup, Others 2
Debut:	League, 31 August 1946 v Arsenal (h) won 6–1
Also played for:	Oakengates Town, Walsall, Wellington Town, Oswestry Town, Cambridge United, GKN Sankeys, England (3 caps)
Managed:	Wellington Town

Johnny Hancocks played mainly on the right wing but could also occupy the left flank just as well. At 5ft 3in, he was on the short size for a footballer of his generation, but with the heart of a lion and guts of a tiger he made up for a lack of inches with some tremendous displays, some unbelievable shooting and a never-say-die attitude, thrilling the Wolves supporters for a decade to become part of Molineux folklore.

As a youngster, keen on football, Hancocks played at centre-half and inside-left, and after representing the Wrekin Schools team he made his debut for Oakengates Town in the Birmingham League at the age of 15. He developed fast and in October 1938 signed as a professional for Walsall. In 1940 he joined the Army and became a Physical Training Instructor, something he knew a lot about from his days running round the Fellows Park pitch and doing fitness exercises in the gym.

During the war Hancocks played in several representative games and also guested for Shrewsbury Town and Wrexham before he made his last appearance for Walsall against Bournemouth in the Third Division South Cup Final at Stamford Bridge in May 1946, which the Saddlers lost 1–0. A week later Wolves, rebuilding for the start of the first peacetime League season, paid £4,000 for his signature. And what a terrific signing he turned out to be.

After getting acquainted with his new teammates on a summer tour of Sweden, Hancocks got down to business by helping destroy Arsenal 6–1 on his Molineux debut, with another fresh face, Jessie Pye, scoring a hat-trick before a 51,000 crowd. The Molineux fans took to him immediately as his dazzling displays down the right wing turned experienced left-backs inside out.

In mid-October 1946 Hancocks claimed his first Wolves goal in another 6–1 win, this time over Huddersfield. Absent from only two games in his first season of top-flight football, he was a shade disappointed when Wolves lost the title to Liverpool on the very last day. The following season the fans marvelled at his powerhouse shooting from free-kicks and penalties as he ended up as joint top scorer with Pye on 16 goals.

In December 1948 Hancocks gained the first of three full England caps, netting twice in a 6–0 win over Switzerland at Highbury. His other outings followed against Wales in 1949 and Yugoslavia in 1950, and he also represented the Football League on two occasions. He collected his first club medal in 1949, helping Wolves beat Leicester 3–1 in the FA Cup Final, but, after finishing third, fifth and sixth in the three respective peacetime seasons, Portsmouth took the League title on goal average from Wolves in 1950.

At the start of the new decade, Wolves' fortunes began to slip, and despite Johnny's 19 goals, including his first hat-trick for the club in a 3–1 win over West Bromwich Albion, they dropped down to 14th and also lost to Newcastle in an FA Cup semi-final replay. Following one bad and one good season, in 1953–54 Wolves, at last, won the League title they had been chasing for 20 years, six players sharing 96 goals with Hancocks scoring 24, and included in his tally was another hat-trick in an 8–1 drubbing of Chelsea. Wolves finished runners-up again in 1954–55, Johnny heading the scoring charts with 27 goals, one of which came in a thrilling 4–4 Charity Shield draw with Albion. After netting 18 times in 1955–56 – and to the chagrin of the Molineux faithful – he surprisingly lost his place in the team when Stan Cullis signed Harry Hooper. He spent a season in the reserves before taking over as player-manager of Wellington Town in 1958. Two years later he joined Cambridge United and later assisted Oswestry Town and GKN Sankeys, finally taking off his size-three boots in 1961.

Employed in an Oakengates iron foundry until 1979, he attended regular functions involving ex-Wolves players before ill health took a hold. He was 74 when he died in 1994.

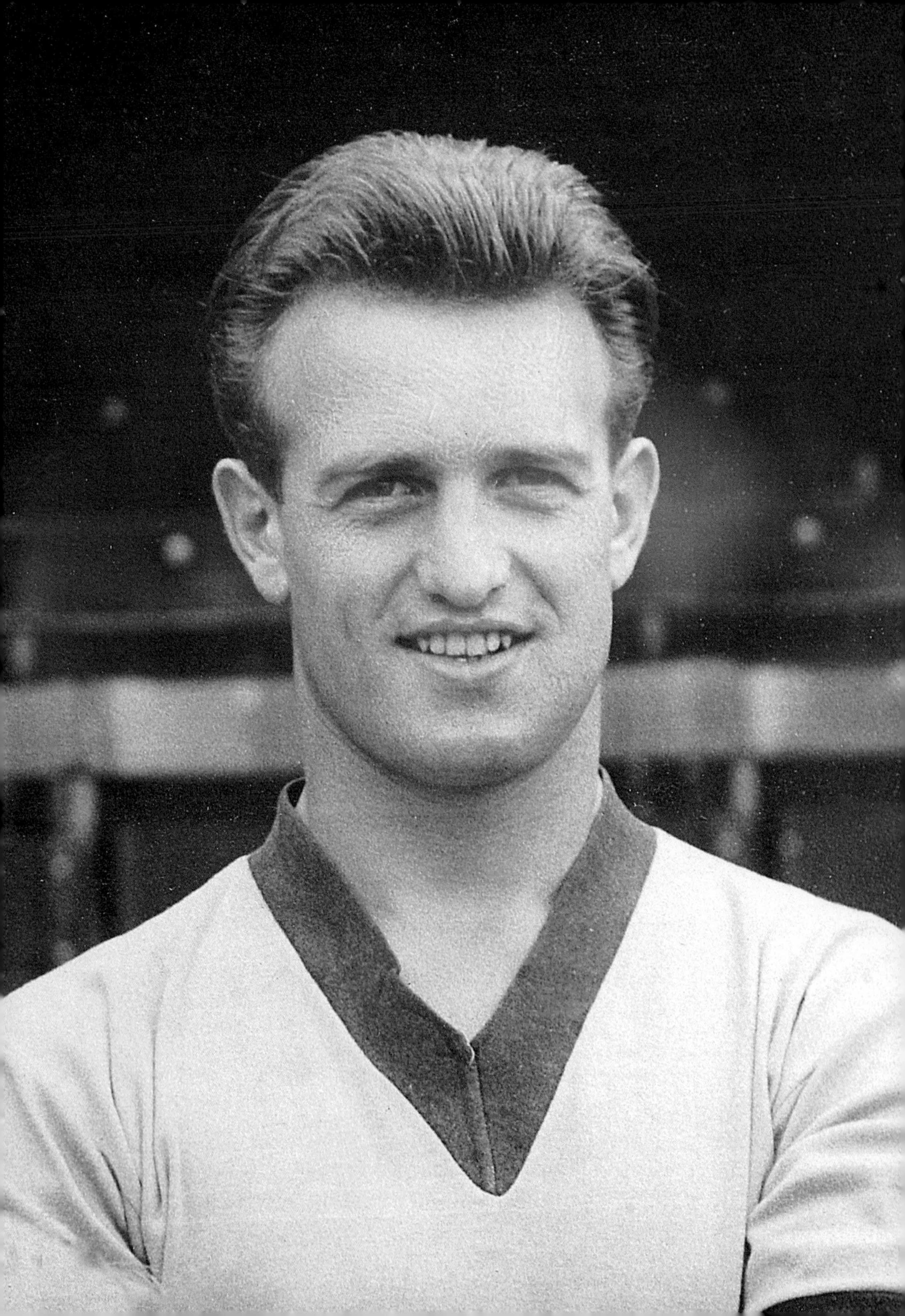

GERRY HARRIS

Date of birth: 8 October 1935, Claverley near Bridgnorth

Wolves record:
Appearances: League 235, FA Cup 24, Europe 9, Others 2
Goals: League 2, FA Cup 0, Europe 0, Others 0
Debut: League, 29 August 1956 v Luton Town (h) won 5–4

Also played for: Walsall, England (4 Under-23 caps)

Gerry Harris was playing as a left-winger for Bobbington FC in the Wolverhampton Amateur League when he went for a trial with West Bromwich Albion. He failed to impress the onlookers at The Hawthorns and soon afterwards was spotted by Wolves scout George Noakes, who immediately referred him to manager Stan Cullis at Molineux. Within a couple of weeks he had signed amateur forms for Wolves, and after making excellent progress through the youth and intermediate ranks he was handed a professional contract in January 1954.

Converted into a left-back, Harris had to work hard at his game, and with so many other players available for selection in the same position he had to wait another two and a half years before making his League debut against Luton Town in a nine-goal thriller under the lights at Molineux, when he deputised for Bill Shorthouse.

Five weeks later Shorthouse was injured and Harris took over the number-three shirt on a regular basis. He never looked back, went from strength to strength and became recognised as one of the finest attacking left-backs Wolves had had for many years. He formed an excellent partnership with Eddie Stuart and was outstanding when Wolves won the League title for the second time in the club's history in 1958, Gerry missing only three games. The following season he was absent twice as the Championship was retained, and this season saw him score the first of his two goals for Wolves, a cracker in a 3–3 draw against Burnley at Molineux.

Strong and mobile with a good turn of foot, Harris was a fine tackler, kicked well and was quick to regain his position. Very few wingers got the better of him for pace, and, in fact, very few gave him the run a round. Two players he admitted he didn't like playing against were Stanley Matthews and Tom Finney...but that could be said of a lot of full-backs!

After gaining successive League Championship-winning medals with Wolves in the later 1950s, Harris added an FA Cup-winners' prize to his collection after Blackburn Rovers had been beaten 3–0 in the 1960 Final. He had a fine game that afternoon, completely blocking out the threat of England international winger Louis Bimpson. Confident in his own ability, he held his place at left-back the following season, but injuries started to affect his game, and with George Showell and a youthful Bobby Thomson pushing for a place in the side he had to work overtime to stay in contention.

When Eddie Stuart left Molineux for Stoke in 1962, manager Stan Cullis replaced him at right-back with Showell, and Thomson was confirmed as his partner, pushing Harris into the reserves where he stayed until the start of the 1964–65 season when he was reinstated at left-back following the departure of Showell and the switching over of Thomson.

Unfortunately that campaign was a disastrous one, Wolves suffering relegation for the first time since 1923. Harris played in 34 League games, but when Cullis left he knew he was on his way out. He remained at Molineux until April 1966 when he joined Walsall, retiring a year later through injury, although he still turned out in charity matches until he was 42.

A keen bowls player, he captained the Bridgnorth club Bylet and today lives in a converted farmhouse in his native Claverley.

BILLY HARRISON

Date of birth:	27 December 1886, Wybunbury, Staffs
Died:	12 August 1948, Wolverhampton

Wolves record:

Appearances:	League 317, FA Cup 28, Wartime 3
Goals:	League 43, FA Cup 6, Wartime 0
Debut:	League, 2 September 1907 v West Bromwich Albion (h) lost 2–1
Also played for:	Hough United, Crewe South End, Willaston White Star, Crewe Alexandra, Stoke (guest), Manchester United, Port Vale, Wrexham

Billy Harrison played outside-right in Wolves' FA Cup-winning team of 1908 when he scored four minutes from time to sew up a 3–1 victory over Newcastle United... And all this happened on the same day his wife gave birth to triplets! That was a wonderful climax to his first season in senior football, having been signed by Wolves from Crewe Alexandra in May 1907 for £400. He went on to have a long and consistent association with Wolves, playing in more than 300 competitive games in a little over nine seasons before leaving Molineux to become successor to the great wing wizard Billy Meredith at Manchester United in October 1920. Billy, who was 34 at the time, was one of three experienced players signed by the club.

Harrison did reasonably well at Old Trafford for two years, but when United were relegated from the top flight in 1922 he was transferred to Port Vale for £250, and after recovering from a broken ankle (suffered in October 1922) he switched to Wrexham for £300 in June 1923 and announced his retirement in May 1924 with a total of 411 League appearances to his credit (50 goals).

Blessed with a remarkable turn of speed, Harrison, who was only 5ft 4in tall and weighed just over 11st, became a huge hit with the Molineux faithful, who loved his all-action style, his pace and his trickery. He was two-footed, preferring his right more than his left, was no mean header of the ball despite his height, and he enjoyed a challenge, never flinching or shying away when matched against a bigger and seemingly burlier opponent. He averaged a goal every seven games for Wolves (not bad for an out-and-out winger), but his job was to create rather than score, and over the course of time he certainly laid on opportunities aplenty for his colleagues.

Taking over from Len Williams on the right wing at the start of the 1907–08 campaign, Harrison made 38 appearances in his first season at Molineux, scoring six goals, his first proving to be the winner in the Christmas Day home League game against Gainsborough Trinity (1–0). He also netted twice in Wolves' FA Cup run. He missed three games in each of the following two seasons through injury and was absent on five occasions in 1910–11 before having two successive ever-present campaigns, when he played quite brilliantly at times as Wolves finished ninth and fifth respectively in Division Two. In 1912–13 he pulled a thigh muscle early on but recovered to add a further 34 appearances to his tally before performing majestically once more in the last two seasons prior to World War One, during which time he assisted Stoke as a guest.

Harrison and Wolves did not have a great 1919–20 campaign. The team struggled desperately out on the pitch, eventually edging clear of relegation by the skin of their teeth. He missed 11 games, the majority through injury, and his displays were well below his normal standard. Nevertheless, he held his place right up until the 10th match of the 1920–21 season when he switched his allegiance to Old Trafford. Wolves took time to find a replacement for him on the right flank, manager Jack Addenbrooke using five different players before finally settling for Sammy Brookes.

After retiring, Billy became an expert crown green bowler, and he was also licensee of the Rose and Crown public house in Tettenhall for many years.

BILLY HARTILL

Date of birth:	18 July 1905, Wolverhampton
Died:	12 August 1980, Walsall

Wolves record:

Appearances:	League, 221, FA Cup 13
Goals:	League 161, FA Cup 8
Debut:	League, 24 November 1928 v Bradford City (a) lost 4–1
Also played for:	Everton, Liverpool, Bristol Rovers

Centre-forward Billy 'Artillery' Hartill was born just a few doors away from his future playing partner Dickie Rhodes, and, as schoolboys, both players represented the Wolverhampton Town side. Having scored literally hundreds of goals at junior level – being a prolific marksman at the age of 10 – he signed up as a bombardier with the Royal Horse Artillery on leaving school, and while in the services he netted more than 70 times in two seasons before he was demobbed.

Wolves signed Hartill as a semi-professional in August 1928, and after making a big impression in the second team Major Frank Buckley blooded him in the first XI at Bradford three months later. He played in the 2–2 home draw with Grimsby Town the following week but then found himself back in the reserves as Wolves struggled to improve their mid-table position in Division Two, and it wasn't until mid-March that he got back into the first team, away at Reading. In his next match he opened his goal account with a brace in a 2–0 win over Chelsea. He was up and running, and after signing as a full-time professional he went from strength to strength after that.

In 1929–30 Hartill cracked in 33 goals in only 36 games. He also struck the first of 16 hat-tricks for the club in a 4–0 home win over Preston, netted a five-timer against Notts County at Molineux and in the penultimate game of the season notched a treble in a 4–4 home draw with Bradford, but overall it turned out to be another poor campaign for Wolves, who finished ninth in the table, six points clear of relegation and 17 adrift of the champions Blackpool.

The following year Wolves edged up to fourth spot as Hartill scored 30 goals in 39 appearances, including another hat-trick in a 9–1 thrashing of Wrexham in the FA Cup. He was now regarded as one of the finest strikers outside the top flight, and in 1931–32 his tally of 30 League goals went a long way in helping Wolves win the Second Division title. He weighed in with four more hat-tricks, against Plymouth Argyle, Bristol City, Southampton and Oldham Athletic, and was mentioned in some quarters as a possible England candidate.

The return to the top flight wasn't a happy one for Wolves, who narrowly escaped the drop, but for hot-shot Hartill the upward move simply improved his form! He reached the century mark in goals for the club and ended the campaign with another 33 in his locker, including a four-timer against Huddersfield Town and hat-tricks against Blackburn Rovers and Derby County in consecutive weeks.

Wolves, as a unit, improved slightly in 1933–34, but surprisingly for Hartill it was not so good. Out injured for a few games, he scored only 13 goals in 27 appearances. But he was back to his lethal best the following season, netting 29 times in 42 games, five coming in a 5–2 Molineux massacre of Aston Villa and another hat-trick against Spurs. Unfortunately that was his last season at Molineux. As Major Buckley began to rebuild his team, he was transferred to Everton, having scored 170 goals, a new club record that was to stand for 46 years, until John Richards topped it in April 1980. After spells with Liverpool and Bristol Rovers, he retired in 1940 with a leg injury.

The ideal centre-forward, Billy could use both foot, was a strong header of the ball and for all his goalscoring efforts the only representative honour that came his way was to play for the Football League against West Bromwich Albion at The Hawthorns in May 1935. This was one of two matches organised to try out an experiment of having two referees to control a game. The Football League beat Albion 9–6, Hartill scoring twice.

SIR JACK HAYWARD

Date of birth: 14 June 1923, Dunstall, Wolverhampton
Wolves: Owner and chairman, 1991 to date

Multi-millionaire businessman Sir Jack Hayward, a Wolves fan since he was a boy, bought the club in May 1990 for £2.1m from Gallagher Estates and immediately placed his son Jonathan and ex-player Billy Wright on the board of directors. He quickly set about redeveloping Molineux and over the next seven years put almost £20m into making the ground a 28,500 all-seater stadium with facilities on a par with most Premiership clubs.

A pupil at Stowe Public School, Hayward used to crawl under the turnstiles to watch Wolves home games in the 1930s. In 1941 he joined the RAF, obtaining his wings after training in Canada and the US. A glider-pilot, taking on the Japanese on the India/Burma border, he was demobbed in 1946 having attained the rank of Flight Lieutenant. After that he worked in South Africa before taking control of his father's business in America.

The business was subsequently moved to the Bahamas, then part of the British Empire, and over the next 42 years this one-time desolate island was converted into one of property and thriving economy, with an efficient airport and seaport, a major tanker terminal and top electrical and water companies all owned by Jack, who also purchased Lundy Island, off the coast of Devon, for the National Trust in 1969 and obtained the first iron ship after the Falkland War, Brunel's SS *Great Britain.* He paid £1m for a hospital in Port Stanley and also made a huge donation to help build MCC's indoor cricket school. And for all his efforts Jack was knighted by the Queen in 1986 at a time when his beloved Wolves were struggling desperately in the Fourth Division.

In March 1994 Sir Jack sacked manager Graham Turner, the man who had previously done wonders by lifting Wolves up from the lower reaches of the Fourth Division into promotion candidates for the Premiership as well as signing Steve Bull. In his place came former England boss Graham Taylor, who was handed £7.5m to spend on new players. But after 18 months in charge he too was dismissed for 'lack of success'.

In May 1997 Sir Jack vowed he would not continue to bail the club out of trouble, claiming it was being run 'sloppily'. Four months later he took over as chairman, relegating his son, Jonathan, who had held the position previously, to vice-chairman. He also brought in another ex-player, John Richards, as managing director. Four weeks after taking the chair, he paid off the club's £8m bank overdraft, and later in the year it was revealed that he had forked out around £40m from his own account to keep Wolves going.

In March 1998 Sir Jack underwent a triple heart bypass in Los Angeles. He recovered in time to see Wolves lose to Arsenal in that year's FA Cup semi-final, but four months into the next season he sacked manager Mark McGhee, appointing Colin Lee as caretaker manager, making the position permanent later.

Confident that Premiership football would soon be seen at Molineux, Sir Jack revealed in January 1999 that he had filed papers at the High Court, suing his son Jonathan, solicitor James Nicholas Stones and his firm Wiggin & Company, of which he is the senior tax partner, over alleged financial irregularities totalling £237,400. The action surrounded the movement of monies within the club without authority from Sir Jack when Jonathan was chairman. Sir Jack was successful.

With nothing forthcoming on the playing side, manager Lee left halfway through the 2000–01 season and into his place stepped Dave Jones, backed all the way by Sir Jack, who had also earlier replaced John Richards with Jez Moxey. Sir Jack was on a high when Wolves reached the First Division Play-offs in 2002, but his joy quickly turned to despair as Norwich City won the two-leg semi-final. Obviously disappointed, he kept faith with Jones, and a year later he was overcome with joy as Wolves finally made it into the top flight, beating Sheffield United 3–0 in the Play-off Final.

Unfortunately Wolves spent only one season with the big boys, after that Glenn Hoddle took over as manager and his second son Rick Hayward as chairman. But, to be honest, Sir Jack – said to be the world's 125th richest man – would love to see Wolves back in, and even win, the Premiership before he calls it a day.

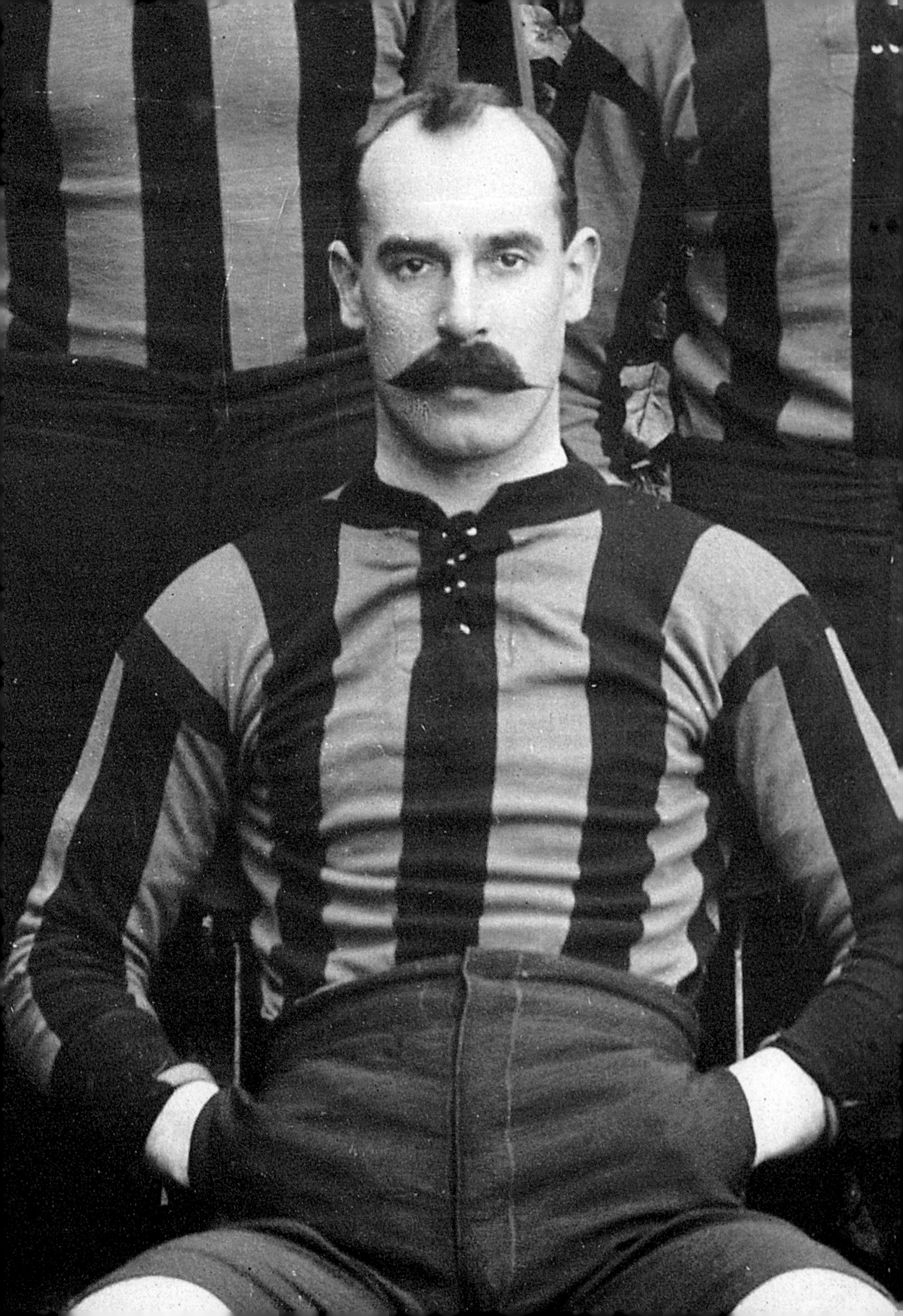

GEORGE HEDLEY

Date of birth: 20 July 1876, South Bank, Northumberland
Died: 16 August 1942, Wolverhampton

Wolves record:
Appearances: League 193, FA Cup 21
Goals: League 65, FA Cup 9
Debut: League, 1 September 1906 v Hull City (h) drew 1–1

Also played for: South Bank, Sheffield United, Southampton
Managed: Bristol City

Popular with teammates and spectators alike, robust, opportunist centre-forward George Hedley, very much an advocate of the open game (a belief he pleaded in a newspaper article in 1909), was considered something of a veteran at the time of his joining relegated Wolves in May 1906. Nevertheless, he quickly formed a robust partnership with Billy Woodridge and then Jack Gorman, as secretary-manager Jack Addenbrooke set about formulating a side capable of making a rapid return to the top flight.

With his first club Sheffield United, whom he joined initially as an amateur in 1897 from his home-town club South Bank, Hedley, who seemed to glory in Cup football, had gained two FA Cup-winners' medals, the first in 1899 against Derby County and the second in 1902 against Southampton, when he scored. He received his one and only England international cap in March 1901, starring in a 3–0 win over Ireland at his future home The Dell, and he also represented the Football League.

It was by accident that he came to leave Bramall Lane for Southampton in May 1903. Having torn heart muscles, it was thought that Hedley's footballing days were numbered. However, with no transfer fees between the Football and Southern Leagues, he went against doctor's orders, accepted an invitation to move to The Dell, and went on playing for another 10 years.

Hedley did exceptionally well with the Saints, for whom he scored 34 goals in 80 appearances over a period of three years, helping them win the Southern League title before his surprise switch to Molineux, surprising in as much as he seemed very happy and settled at Southampton. But someone at Wolves must have had a midas touch in persuading him to leave the south coast for the industrial Black Country. He served Wolves superbly well for seven years, gaining a third FA Cup-winners' medal in 1908 when he scored in a 3–1 win over Newcastle United in the Final at Crystal Palace. That game was unusual as the surnames of all four goalscorers began with the letter 'H'.

In his first season at Molineux, Hedley, who packed a ferocious right-foot shot and could head a ball as hard as some players could kick one, netted 11 goals in 38 competitive games, his haul including a brilliant hat-trick in a 6–2 home League win over Burslem Port Vale. He was top scorer with 16 goals in 1907–08 when Wally Radford was his main strike-partner, and the following season, despite suffering a series of niggling injury problems, he netted 12 times as Wolves struggled to get into a position from where they could challenge for promotion. Besides leading the attack, he also played in both inside-forward positions, and in 1909–10, when he claimed 10 goals, two-thirds of his appearances were made at inside-left. In 1910–11, when he struck 13 goals, he had Jack Needham as his partner-in-crime up front, and in his last two seasons as a Wolves player he was ably-assisted by Needham and Billy Halligan before Albert Groves was brought into the side in place of Hedley during the second half of the 1912–13 campaign.

After his retirement at the age of 36, in April 1913, Hedley had a brief two-season managerial flirtation with Bristol City, guiding them to eighth and 13th places in the Second Division. A licensee in Bristol for 23 years, from 1918 to 1941, George was looking after a boarding house in Wolverhampton when he died at the age of 66 after a short illness.

It is said that George wore the same pair of boots for 10 years, and when he finally discarded them (soon after the 1908 Cup Final) they had 17 patches on them – yet, even then, still fitted like a glove!

WW

KENNY HIBBITT

Date of birth: 3 January 1951, Bradford, West Yorkshire

Wolves record:
Appearances: League 447+19, FA Cup 46+1, League Cup 35+1, European 16+1, Others 8
Goals: League 89, FA Cup 10, League Cup 12, European 3, Others 0
Debut: League, 12 September 1970 v Chelsea (a) drew 2–2

Also played for: Bradford Park Avenue, Coventry City, Bristol Rovers (player and assistant manager)
Managed: Walsall, Cardiff City (also coach and director of football)

Kenny Hibbitt starred in the Wolves midfield for 16 years, amassing a fine record of 544 senior appearances and scoring 114 goals – a terrific return for a player in his position. A snip of a signing by manager Ronnie Allen, who paid just £5,000 for his signature from Bradford in November 1968, after he had played in just 15 League games for the Yorkshire club, he had to wait until September 1970 before making his debut, scoring to celebrate the occasion in a 2–2 draw against the reigning FA Cup holders Chelsea at Stamford Bridge. By this time Allen had been replaced as manager by Bill McGarry, who stated that he was 'An inspirational player, a player who gives nothing less than 100 percent and one who I know will help bring a trophy or two to Molineux.'

Hibbitt played in 37 first-team games in 1970–71, helping Wolves win the Texaco Cup when they defeated Heart of Midlothian over two legs in a very close Final. The following season he was in the Wolves team that lost to Tottenham Hotspur in the UEFA Cup Final (after another close contest), and in 1972–73, when he produced some superb performances, he and Wolves came within a whisker of reaching both the FA Cup and League Cup Finals. It was Spurs again who won the two-leg League Cup semi-final and Leeds United who denied the Wanderers their first FA Cup Final appearance for 13 years, winning the semi-final clash 1–0 at Maine Road. However, after all that disappointment, Hibbitt, at long last, won a major prize at Wolves, his opening goal paving the way for a 2–1 victory over Manchester City in the 1974 League Cup Final at Wembley.

The driving force in centre-field, Hibbitt and his captain Mike Bailey were in terrific form throughout that season and again in 1974–75 when he netted all his side's goals in a 4–2 home League win over Newcastle United, but, for all their efforts, Kenny's in particular, Wolves were relegated to the Second Division at the end of the 1975–76 campaign. This came as a huge shock to everyone at Molineux, but, thankfully, under the management of Sammy Chung, promotion was gained at the first attempt, Kenny top-scoring with 18 goals (17 in the League).

Hibbitt played his part in helping the team re-establish itself in the top flight but suffered disappointment again in 1979 when Wolves lost 1–0 to Arsenal in another FA Cup semi-final. Thankfully all was forgotten 12 months later as Wolves returned to Wembley and lifted the League Cup for the second time in six years by beating Nottingham Forest 1–0.

Another FA Cup semi-final defeat followed in 1981 and after a second relegation and immediate promotion, plus a well-deserved testimonial, Hibbitt left Molineux for Coventry City, switching to Bristol Rovers in 1986. When he returned to Molineux as Rovers' coach in 1989 the South Bank saluted him in recognition of the magnificent service he had given to their club. His illustrious playing career had come to a sad end in February 1988 when he broke a leg playing for Rovers against Sunderland. As assistant to Gerry Francis, he helped the Bristol club win the Third Division title and reach the Leyland DAF Final, and later, as manager of Walsall, he steered the Saddlers into the Third Division Play-offs. In 1995 he became Cardiff City's new manager and later assumed the role of coach and then director of football at Ninian Park.

A member of the Wolves Former Players' Association, Kenny is currently living in Gloucestershire. His brother Terry played in midfield for Newcastle United, Leeds United and Birmingham City but died of cancer in 1994, aged 46.

REG HOLLINGWORTH

Date of birth: 17 October 1909, Rainworth near Mansfield
Died: 8 July 1969, Sparkbrook, Birmingham

Wolves record:
Appearances: League 167, FA Cup 13
Goals: League 7, FA Cup 1
Debut: League, 10 November 1928 v West Bromwich Albion (a) won 2–0

Also played for: Nuffield Colliery, Sutton Junction

Centre-half Reg Hollingworth was one of the unluckiest footballers ever to play for Wolves. He was plagued by a series of leg, hip and back injuries, was out of action for long periods through illness, suffered concussion on three occasions, twice dislocated his shoulder, had over a dozen stitches in various head wounds, and in March 1932, having been selected to play for England against The Rest in an international trial at Huddersfield, ahead of the senior game against Scotland at Wembley the following month, he damaged his ankle playing for Wolves in a League game at Barnsley. He sat out the trial match and as a result his place in the full England team went to Peter O'Dowd of Chelsea. Sadly, he was never considered again, not even as a reserve. Four years later he suffered another crucial injury and this one ended his career, Reg announcing his retirement, reluctantly, at the age of 27, although he did continue playing in local charity matches for quite some time.

Tall and strong, solid in the tackle and a good, clean header and kicker of the ball, Hollingworth was blessed with all the right attributes a defender requires. He did well in local intermediate football before joining Wolves as a professional in November 1928, making his debut in the Black Country against neighbours West Bromwich Albion just 48 hours after signing. He was recruited following an injury to Tom Pritchard and played in 10 League games (won four) before dropping into the reserves, returning to first-team action in September 1929 and again at the end of that season before finally claiming a regular place in the half-back line at the start of the 1930–31 campaign, when he had, as his two wing-halves, George Lax and Dai Richards, the former eventually giving way to Dicky Rhodes.

Hollingworth scored the first of his eight goals in a 3–1 home League win over Reading in October 1930, securing his second in a 3–2 home win over Southampton at the end of January 1931. He very rarely ventured into opposing penalty-areas, but when he did he was always a threat in the air, and in one game, against Bury, his presence in the 18-yard box led to two goals. Wolves won the Second Division title in 1931–32, Reg playing in 32 of the 42 League games. He was outstanding at times and contributed four more goals, one a vital strike in a 3–3 draw at Plymouth.

Unfortunately, after that triumph injuries started to affect his game. He made only 12 appearances in 1932–33 and 15 the following season, before regaining full fitness for the 1934–35 campaign when he was switched to right-back after an injury to Wilf Lowton. He didn't particularly like playing there, but he still gave some impressive displays before injury struck again in the home game with Leeds United in November 1935. Unfortunately, he never recovered form this set-back, and despite a strenuous fitness programme he quit the game within six months and subsequently joined the Staffordshire Police Force. He later took employment at the Goodyear tyre factory (Wolverhampton) before becoming manager of Batchelor Robinson and Company in Balsall Heath, a position he held for 22 years, until his tragic death from a heart attack in 1969.

JOHN HOLSGROVE

Date of birth: 27 September 1945, Southwark, Middlesex

Wolves record:
Appearances: League 178+2, FA Cup 10, League Cup 8, Others 4
Goals: League 7, FA Cup 0, League Cup 0, Others 0
Debut: League, 25 September 1965 v Bury (h) won 3–0

Also played for: Arsenal, Tottenham Hotspur, Crystal Palace, Sheffield Wednesday

A tall, powerfully-built defender, John Holsgrove proved to be a wonderful signing by Wolves manager Andy Beattie, who paid just £18,000 for his services from Crystal Palace in May 1965 – this after he had been recommended to Wolves by the then Palace player-coach Ronnie Allen, who two months later would become John's boss. Registered as an amateur at both Highbury and White Hart Lane, he signed as an apprentice at Selhurst Park in April 1962 and turned professional on his 18th birthday.

A former England Youth international, Holsgrove made only 22 senior appearances for Palace and began his Wolves career in the reserves before gaining a place in the first team at the end of September 1965 – just after Allen had replaced Beattie as manager following a crushing 9–3 defeat at Southampton. Taking over from Scotsman George Miller at left-half, he played in 25 games that season, scoring two goals, both coming in an 8–2 home League win over Portsmouth. The following season he and centre-half Dave Woodfield were brilliant at the back as Wolves reclaimed their position in the top flight, taking the runners'-up spot behind Coventry City after an excellent campaign that saw John appear in 25 League and five Cup matches, adding one more goal to his tally in a 3–1 win at Carlisle.

An ever present in his first season of Division One football, Holsgrove produced some terrific performances at the heart of the defence, finding time to venture forward and knock in four goals, clinching victory at Arsenal and saving a point at home to Newcastle. He went on to have an unbroken run in the first team of almost 100 matches before being ruled out of a fourth-round FA Cup tie at Tottenham in February 1969. He returned to the team as confident as ever and was eventually switched to centre-half by new manager Bill McGarry when first John McAlle (from March 1969) and then Frank Munro (from August 1969) were introduced to the defence. Looking composed and comfortable on the ball, John was strong in the air and possessed a telling tackle, hardly ever being reckless with his challenges.

As time rolled by McGarry brought back McAlle and switched Munro into the middle of the defence, meaning, in effect, that Holsgrove's career at Molineux was over. One or two clubs were interested in signing him, but in the end he chose Sheffield Wednesday, joining for the Owls in a £50,000 deal in June 1971, having made more than 200 senior appearances for Wolves.

Holsgrove spent four seasons at Hillsborough, during which time he made a further 115 appearances before rounding off his career with Stockport County, retiring through injury in the summer of 1976. John now works as a financial advisor in the West Midlands. A very useful guitarist, he was a good friend of pop star Lulu, and his son Paul played for Aldershot and Luton Town and had loan spells with Wimbledon, West Bromwich Albion and Stoke City among others.

EMLYN HUGHES, OBE

Date of birth: 28 August 1947, Barrow-in-Furness
Died: 9 November 2004, Sheffield

Wolves record:
Appearances: League 56+2, FA Cup 5, League Cup 12, Europe 2
Goals: League 2, FA Cup 0, League Cup 0, Europe 0
Debut: League, 21 August 1979 v Derby County (a) won 1–0

Also played for: Blackpool, Liverpool, Rotherham United, Hull City, Mansfield Town, Swansea City, England (8 Under-23 and 62 full caps)
Managed: Rotherham United

Emlyn Hughes had a wonderful career in football that spanned almost 20 years. He represented North Lancashire Schools and Roose FC (Blackpool) before joining Blackpool as a professional in September 1964. Two and a half years later he moved to Liverpool for £65,000 and made 665 senior appearances for the Merseyside club, up to August 1979, when he was signed by Wolves manager John Barnwell for £90,000. He spent two seasons at Molineux, and after spells with Rotherham United (player-manager from July 1981), Hull City (from March 1983), Mansfield Town (from August 1983) and Swansea City (September-October 1983) he announced his retirement through injury.

Nicknamed 'Crazy Horse', he was, without doubt, a terrific footballer who played for the love of the game. Tough and resilient, he never shirked a tackle, always gave 100 percent out on the field, for club and country, and, as one scribe wrote, '...he was strong, durable and courageous, the soul of consistency, never ruffled, with a big heart, a tenacious player of the bulldog breed.'

Hughes made his League debut for Liverpool in the unfamiliar number-10 shirt in 1967. After that he played at left-back, left-half, in midfield and as an emergency central-defender. The scorer of some spectacular goals, many from a distance, he captained the Reds many times and during his time at Anfield won both the European Cup and UEFA Cup twice, the European Super Cup once, gained four League Championship-winning medals in six years between 1973 and 1979, won the FA Cup and twice lifted the Charity Shield. He was also voted FWA Player of the Year in 1977.

A real snip of a signing by Wolves, Hughes replaced John McAlle at the heart of the defence and appeared in 33 League and 13 Cup games in his first season with the club, returning to Wembley to lead the team to a 1–0 League Cup Final victory over Nottingham Forest. He formed an excellent defensive barrier at Molineux with Welsh international George Berry alongside him, flanked by full-backs Geoff Palmer and Derek Parkin. His encouragement and drive made him a great favourite with the fans, and some say at times he played better in his second season with the club than he did in his first, despite Wolves slipping down to 18th in the League table. Eventually switched to left-half following the return of John McAlle, he chose to move on at the end of the 1981–82 campaign, having contributed a lot to Wolves' cause in a relatively short period of time.

Capped 62 times by England at senior level (over a period of 10 years: 1970–80), Hughes also played in eight Under-21 internationals and represented the Football League. He accumulated well over 900 appearances at club and international level and after retiring became a TV personality, captaining one of the teams in *A Question of Sport*. He sadly died of cancer at the age of 57. His father was a Rugby League international who played for Barrow, his brother and uncle also played rugby, while his aunt represented England at women's hockey.

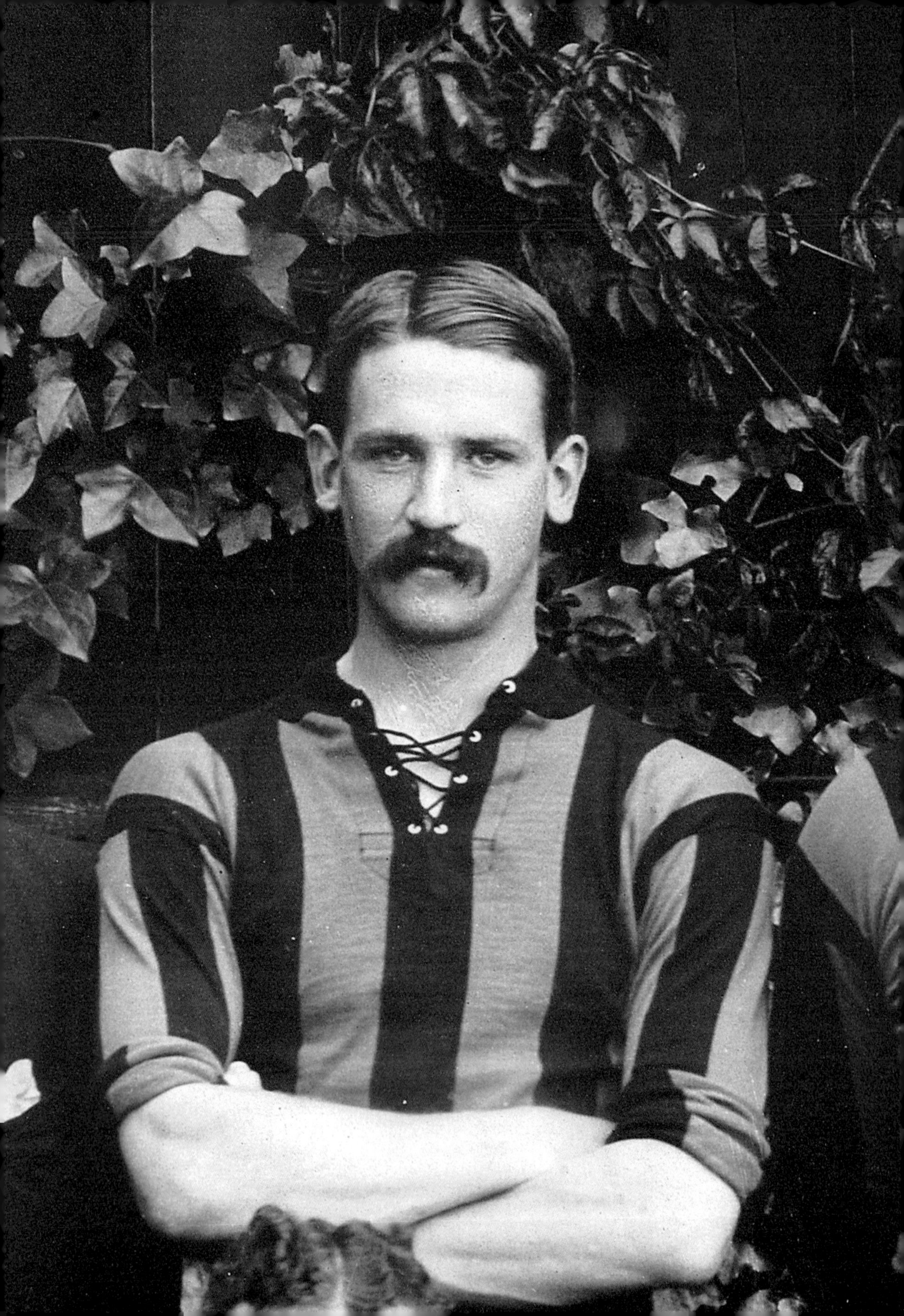

KENNETH HUNT (Reverend)

Date of birth: 24 February 1884, Oxford
Died: 28 April 1949, Oxford

Wolves record:
Appearances: League 50, FA Cup 11
Goals: League 1, FA Cup 1
Debut: League, 23 March 1907 v Burnley (h) won 3–0

Also played for: Trent College, Queen's College (Oxford), Oxford City, Crystal Palace, Oxford University, Corinthians, England (2 full and 20 amateur caps)

The Reverend Kenneth Hunt played for Wolverhampton Boys Grammar School for four years at the turn of the 20th century, and after spells with several amateur and university teams he starred in a practice match at Molineux in March 1907, and Wolves immediately registered him as a player. A right-half, he made his debut soon afterwards in the 3–0 home League win over Burnley and had two further outings that season when it was plain to see that Wolves had acquired a brilliant footballer. Unfortunately the Reverend Hunt could not be lured away on a permanent basis from his studies at Oxford University, much to the disappointment of the Wolves board.

However, the following season Hunt managed to appear in 21 League games, helping Wolves rise to ninth in the Second Division table, while at the same time he performed magnificently in the FA Cup competition, playing in all seven matches. In a third-round replay against Bradford Park Avenue, a crowd of almost 14,000 saw the Reverend Hunt inspire Wolves to a 1–0 home win, George Hedley putting the finishing touch to a move started by him. After home victories over Bury and Swindon in rounds four and five, Wolves travelled to the Potteries for a quarter-final clash with Stoke. Ken played superbly well, as did the rest of the team, in a 1–0 win to set up a semi-final clash with Southampton. Inspired yet again by the bold efforts of their muscular vicar, Wolves pulled out all the stops to beat the Saints 2–0 with goals from Hedley and Wally Radford. In the Final Wolves took on and defeated Newcastle United 3–1 in front of almost 75,000 spectators at Crystal Palace. It became known as the 'H' Final, with Wolves' three goals coming from Harrison, Hedley and the Reverend Hunt. Jim Howie netted for the hot favourites United.

Wolves' triumph went down as a major upset, and the Reverend's 40th-minute goal came from 25 yards, the ball fizzing through 'keeper Jimmy Lawrence's fingers and into the roof of the net. This was the first of only two goals he scored for Wolves – his second followed in a 2–1 home League win over Leeds City 12 months later.

An FA Cup-winners' medal wasn't the Reverend's only reward that year. He collected his Oxford Blue and also gained a gold medal as Great Britain won the Olympic Games soccer tournament in London.

Spending a lot of time playing for Leyton and Oxford City, and only journeying to Wolverhampton when his studies allowed, his time at Molineux was now being regarded as an exception rather than a rule. He played only 12 times for Wolves in 1908–09 and made nine appearances the following season. After that he was rarely seen, and over a period of three years, from August 1910 to April 1913, he participated in just eight first-class matches while also appearing in the FA Amateur Cup Final for Oxford City. After the hostilities of World War One, he played in one more League game for Wolves, helping them beat Stoke 4–0 at Molineux in the penultimate game of the 1919–20 season.

An amateur throughout his career, the Reverend Hunt gained 20 caps for England at this level (1907–20) as well as playing twice for the senior side, against Wales and Scotland in 1911.

Ordained in 1909, the Reverend Hunt became housemaster at Highgate School, London, where he was heavily involved in public schools soccer until 1945. He served on the FA Council from 1946 to 1949, when he retired through ill health – 48 hours after Wolves had beaten Leicester City in the FA Cup Final.

Although he made only 61 appearances for Wolves, Kenneth Reginald Gunnery Hunt – a striking personality who was absolutely without fear – is one of Wolves' all-time greats. A collection of his caps, medals and other memorabilia are on display in the Molineux trophy cabinet.

Doritos

PAUL INCE

Date of birth: 21 October 1967, Ilford, Essex

Wolves record:
Appearances: League 107+7, FA Cup 8, League Cup 4+1, Others 3
Goals: League 10, FA Cup 1, League Cup 1, Others 0
Debut: League, 17 September 2002, substitute v Burnley (h) won 3–0

Also played for: West Ham United, Manchester United, Inter Milan, Liverpool, Middlesbrough, England (2 Under-21, 1 B and 53 full caps)

Everywhere he's played, Paul Ince has done a tremendous job in midfield. Strong-running, hard-working, full of heart and energy with no mean skill, blessed with a powerful right-foot shot and a never-say-die approach, he made his mark with West Ham, for whom he appeared in 95 senior games before transferring to Manchester United for £1m in September 1989.

The scorer of 29 goals in 281 outings during six seasons at Old Trafford, Ince then joined Italian giants Inter Milan for £8m in July 1995, switching to Liverpool for £4.2m two years later after making 54 appearances in Serie A. In two seasons at Anfield he played in 81 competitive matches, and, following his move to the Riverside Stadium for £1m in August 1999, he starred in 106 first-class games for Middlesbrough before joining Wolves of a free transfer in August 2002.

At the time of his arrival at Molineux, Ince had already been a professional for 17 years and had accumulated in excess of 660 club and international appearances (82 goals scored) while gaining nine medals, all with Manchester United between 1991 and 1994, for two Premiership titles, two FA Cup wins, a European Cup-winners' Cup victory, European Super Cup success, a League Cup win and glory in two Charity Shield matches. He was also an experienced international, and, having represented England as a youth-team player, he went on to win two Under-21, one B and 53 full caps for his country, featuring in the European Championships in 1996 and the World Cup Finals two years later. He was also voted runner-up to Paul McGrath in the PFA Player of the Year poll in 1993.

After gaining full fitness, Ince's sheer presence lifted Wolves, his encouragement and experience showing through as he replaced Paul Butler as captain. Competitive from the word go, he played in 45 out of 55 games in his first season at Molineux, helping Wolves gain a place in the Premiership via the Play-offs. He admitted he wasn't at his best in 2003–04 when Wolves were relegated, but he still managed to play in another 35 games, and then, the following season, he reached the century mark in appearances for the club while at the same time edging past the milestone of 700 games at club level in his career.

Even at the age of 38, Ince was still grafting away in midfield, urging his colleagues on and always giving a good and honest account of himself, no matter what the circumstances or match, but Ince has now left Wolves after the arrival of new manager Mick McCarthy.

Paul's cousin is the former boxing champion Nigel Benn.

BRYN JONES

Date of birth: 2 February 1912, Penyard, Merthyr Tydfil
Died: 18 October 1985, Wood Green, London

Wolves record:
Appearances: League 163, FA Cup 52
Goals: League 52, FA Cup 5
Debut: League, 18 November 1933 v Everton (a) won 2–1

Also played for: Merthyr Amateurs, Plymouth United, Southend United (trial), Glenavon, Aberaman, Arsenal, Norwich City, Wales (17 caps)

Bryn Jones's soccer career began at Queens Road school, Merthyr. At the age of 14 he took virtually the only option open to him for work, which was to go down the pit. Playing in the local South Wales District League, he had an unsuccessful trial with Southend before joining the Irish club Glenavon (1932). In August 1933 he returned to Wales to play for Aberaman and three months later signed for Wolves in a £1,500 deal.

Jones's League debut came 72 hours later, away to the FA Cup holders Everton. He did well in a 2–1 victory but was dropped for the next game, only to return the following Saturday when he scored his first goal for Wolves in a 3–1 defeat at Derby. He didn't miss another game that season, netting 10 goals in 27 appearances as Wolves finished a disappointing 15th in the First Division table. The following season he played in all but nine games, and although claiming only seven goals he endeared himself to the Wolves supporters with his excellent ball control and unselfish play. In fact, he set up several goals for his colleagues – far more than he scored himself. For Wolves it was to prove another fruitless year as they finished in the lower reaches of the top division once more, yet Jones's obvious skills were recognised, and he was chosen to play for Wales against Northern Ireland – winning the first of 17 full caps.

On the domestic front, however, he had to work overtime in a rather mediocre Wolves side that once again finished a disappointing 15th in the table in 1935–36. He missed just two games that year and hit nine goals, including his first-ever hat-trick at senior level at Molineux against Preston shortly before the season's end. He represented his country against Northern Ireland, Scotland and England, the latter game taking place on his home patch, Molineux, when he scored in a shock 2–1 win for Wales.

The goals netted by Tom Galley, Gordon Clayton and Jones helped Wolves achieve some respectability in 1936–37 when the team rose to fifth place in the League while also reaching the quarter-finals of the FA Cup. In-form Bryn scored 14 times in 33 appearances and won three more caps, against England, Ireland and Scotland. He starred against the same three countries the following season when he was quite outstanding, his magic in centre field helping Wolves take the runners'-up spot behind Arsenal... and if they had beaten Sunderland in their final game they would have won the Championship. He missed half a dozen games and scored 17 more goals, but soon after there was an outcry from the fans when, in August 1938, he was transferred to Arsenal for the then record British fee of £14,000. Such was the popularity of the 5ft 6in tall Welshman that there was a four-hour demonstration outside Molineux when he left.

Continuing to win caps with the Gunners, for whom he appeared in 76 first-class games, Jones served in the 34th Light AA Regiment in North Africa and Italy during the war, and he stayed at Highbury until 1949 when he was appointed player-coach of Norwich City. After two seasons with the Canaries, his doctor advised him to quit the game because of a chest condition. Returning to London, he ran a newsagent-tobacconist shop in Stoke Newington near Highbury from September 1951 to April 1979.

Jones had four footballing brothers: Ivor (ex-WBA, Swansea Town and Wales), Bill (Merthyr Town), Emlyn (Merthyr, Everton and Southend) and Bert (Southend and Wolves). He was also the uncle of Cliff Jones (ex-Spurs and Wales).

JACK JONES

Date of birth:	16 March 1877, Wellington, Salop
Died:	10 August 1945, Wolverhampton

Wolves record:

Appearances:	League 314, FA Cup 22, Wartime 6
Goals:	League 16, FA Cup 0, Wartime 0
Debut:	League, 2 September 1901 v Nottingham Forest (h) won 2–0
Also played for:	Wrockwardine Wood, Lanesfield FC

Full-back Jackery Jones was born in the same year Wolves were founded (1877). He learnt the game playing local intermediate football in his native county before moving to Molineux as a senior professional at the age of 23. He had to bide his time in Wolves' second team in 1900–01 before gaining a place in the first XI the following campaign. Taking over from Harry Davies, he made the first of 336 senior appearances against Nottingham Forest at the start of the 1901–02 season, partnering George Walker in a 2–0 win in front of just 4,000 supporters.

An ever present in each of his first three League campaigns as a senior Wolves player, being joined by Dick Betteley in 1902, Jones scored his first two goals for the club during that time, netting in a 4–2 win at Newcastle and a 2–1 victory over Liverpool at Anfield. He took a few knocks in 1904–05 but was up and running within days and missed only three League games that season, being chosen to represent the Football League against the Irish League at Grosvenor Park, Belfast. Absent once in 1905–06, he missed two games the following season and seven in 1907–08 – such was his reliability and consistency. There is no doubt that he was a tough defender, hence his injuries, mainly to his left ankle and both knees. But, as long as he could stand up, invariably he would be available for selection and often went into a game with strapping on one or even both of his legs.

A terrific performer, whose skill complemented a fine physique, Jones was a solid kicker of a ball, clearing his lines efficiently from any angle. He was able to contain the most difficult opponent, never really getting the run around from a winger, and he was always in control of things in tight situations – although he did concede two own-goals during his time at Molineux!

In 1908 Jones starred in Wolves' FA Cup-winning team, playing positively and well at right-back (as always) against a star-studded Newcastle United side who were defeated 3–1 at Crystal Palace, one of his long clearances leading to George Hedley's goal. In January 1910 he became the first Wolves player to appear in 300 League games, and he also holds the record for most ever-present campaigns – five. At this juncture, he was on top of his game, but during the build up to the 1910–11 season he badly twisted his ankle and lost his place at right-back to George Garratly who had played in a few matches the previous season. Garratly comfortably held his position, and as a result Jack managed only three first-team outings up to May 1913 when, at the age 36, he announced his retirement.

Remaining loyal to Wolves, Jones continued to work for the club as assistant trainer (to another ex-player, Albert Fletcher), a position he held until after the war when Elijah Morse arrived on the scene to take over as senior trainer.

A well-known and respected figure at Molineux, Jones, who enjoyed smoking a pipe, always carried his Cup-winners' medal around with him, hanging it proudly from his watch chain attached to his waistcoat pocket. He never refused to show it to those supporters who asked to see it. When Jack died in 1945, part of the club's history went with him. He was a great and wonderful club man.

His brother Joe, also a full-back, played for Wolves from 1898 to 1903.

ALBERT KAY

Date of birth: 22 November 1895, Sheffield
Died: c.1975, Wolverhampton

Wolves record:
Appearances: League 278, FA Cup 17
Goals: League 2, FA Cup 0
Debut: League, 2 September 1922 v Derby County (a) drew 1–1

Also played for: Tinsley FC, Birmingham, Willenhall

Albert Kay was a versatile defender who joined Birmingham immediately after World War One but failed to make the grade at St Andrew's. He returned to non-League football with Willenhall before joining Wolves as a professional in July 1921 as a reserve to Val Gregory, Joe Hodnett, Bill Caddick and Alf Riley.

Kay did well in the Wolves second XI and as a result was handed his senior debut three games into the 1922–23 season at Derby when he replaced Riley at left-half. Retaining his position, he worked hard in a struggling side, and at the end of the campaign, after making 25 League appearances, he and his colleagues were bitterly disappointed when Wolves were relegated to the Third Division North for the first time in the club's history.

With George Jobey at the helm, Wolves tightened up their defence for the following campaign, and Kay started out in the left-half berth with George Getgood and Bill Caddick alongside him in the middle line. From the outset they looked a more solid and confident side, and they held their form throughout the 42-match programme to win the title at the first attempt, Kay missing only four games while also scoring his first goal for the club, the winner at home to Crewe Alexandra in September 1923.

Predominantly a defensive wing-half, Kay could also fill in at full-back if required, and twice in reserve-team games he took over in goal when the regular 'keeper was injured, saving a penalty in the process. He was essentially a gentleman-type of player; not the rugged, tough-tackling, robust defender some teams were blessed with in the 1920s. Few forwards got the better of him, he was hardly ever flustered in tight positions, and, if the truth be told, he loved to be in the thick of the action, his tackling at times being solid and precise.

Temporary manager Albert Hoskins recruited Jack Bradford in the summer of 1924, and as a result Kay, surprisingly in the circumstances, found himself replaced at left-half. He made only nine appearances in the side that season but came back strongly in 1925–26 when Wolves finished a creditable fourth in Division Two, their highest placing since before World War One. Although hard pressed all the way, he retained his place in the half-back line with some resolute performances as Wolves fought for their lives in 1926–27, avoiding relegation by just five points. It was much of the same the next season when again he and his defensive colleagues had to work overtime to collect precious points to stay up.

Over the next three years Kay played his fair share of games, several at left-back following the arrival of Dai Richards, and in 1931–32 he was the recipient of a Second Division Championship medal as the team took the title ahead of Leeds United and Stoke City. This, however, was to be Albert's last season at Molineux. He retired with almost 300 senior appearances under his belt – a worthy effort by any standards.

He stayed local and resided in the Tettenhall and Codsall districts of Wolverhampton before his death in 1975, at the age of 80.

PUMA

ROBBIE KEANE

Date of birth: 8 July 1980, Dublin

Wolves record:
Appearances: League 64+7, FA Cup 3+2, League Cup 7+1
Goals: League 22, FA Cup 2, League Cup 3
Debut: League, August 1999 v Norwich City (a) won 3–2

Also played for: Coventry City, Inter Milan, Leeds United, Tottenham Hotspur, Republic of Ireland (one B, 66 full caps)

Robbie Keane first rose to prominence with Wolves as a 17-year-old when he scored twice on his League debut against Norwich City at Carrow Road on 9 August 1997 – a fortnight after becoming a professional.

Snubbing his boyhood heroes Liverpool because he felt he had a better chance of making a name for himself in the First Division with a lesser-known club, Keane's instincts proved correct, and he was soon banging in the goals for Wolves, ending his first season with 11 under his belt in 45 outings. The following year he top scored with 16 goals in 39 games, netting twice in an FA Cup win at Bolton and grabbing another brace in a 5–0 League Cup victory over Barnet. Sharp, instinctive, quick-witted, with an eye for goal, his form prompted a Premiership bidding war in the summer of 1999, with Aston Villa among the clubs interested in signing him. However, they balked at the £6 million asking price – still a British record for a teenager – while Manchester United boss Alex Ferguson famously declared he'd pay no more than £500,000 and play him in the reserves. In the end, it came down to two clubs – Tottenham Hotspur and Coventry City. He chose the latter, and he instantly silenced his critics by scoring nine Premiership goals before January. But it wasn't just his knack for scoring goals that set him apart, he also drew plaudits for his tireless efforts for the team and unselfish style of play. After his first season at Highfield Road, it was clear that his reputation had spread far and wide when Inter Milan made a £13 million swoop for his services.

It was an offer too good to turn down, and Keane, eager to follow in the footsteps of his fellow countryman Liam Brady, who made a name for himself in Italy, soon had the likes of Ronaldo, Christian Vieri and Clarence Seedorf as his teammates. He made an impressive start in the San Siro and instantly won over the fans. But, when Marcello Lippi – the coach who signed him – was sacked and Marco Tardelli ushered in to replace him, he fell from favour. He was rarely selected and with some reluctance chose to move on, joining Leeds United, initially on loan and later signing permanently for £12 million.

In fact, Leeds had had the chance to sign Keane in his younger days but failed to follow up their interest. It seemed that the Irish contingent at Elland Road – comprising manager O'Leary and players McPhail, Harte and Kelly – was one of the key factors in his decision to join Leeds. He scored some important goals in the first half of 2001, but in his second season he struggled with his form and found himself on the sidelines after the arrival of Robbie Fowler.

At this juncture, Tottenham Hotspur boss Glenn Hoddle stepped in, and Keane completed his 11th-hour transfer to White Hart Lane on the last day of August 2002 for a fee of £7 million.

Keane had earlier made a big impact during the 2002 World Cup Finals, scoring late goals for the Republic of Ireland against Germany and Spain and also finding the net against Saudi Arabia. A natural finisher, he continued to hit the target in his first season with Spurs, a spectacular hat-trick against Everton proving to be the highlight of the campaign. He has since formed excellent partnerships with Fredi Kanoute, Mido and Jermain Defoe and helped Spurs almost reach the Champions League in 2006, while taking his tally of full international caps towards the 70 mark.

In April 2005 Keane was left on the subs' bench in the 1–1 draw with Birmingham. He reacted badly, storming down the tunnel, angry at boss Maarten Jol. He was fined £10,000 by the club and forced to train with the reserves. His future at White Hart Lane looked in doubt, but he quelled all speculation within a short period of time and in 2005–06 turned on the style once more, scoring some stunning goals while taking his career tally in club and international football to an impressive 150.

SPALL
STAW
Sondico

MARK KENDALL

Date of birth: 20 September 1958, Blackwood, Monmouthshire

Wolves record:
Appearances: League 147, FA Cup 5, League Cup 8, Others 17
Goals: 0
Debut: League, 1 January 1987 v Peterborough United (h) lost 3–0

Also played for: Tottenham Hotspur, Chesterfield, Newport County, Swansea City, Newport AFC

Signed by manager Graham Turner halfway through the 1986–87 season after Wolves had used four different goalkeepers over a period of nine months – Tim Flowers, Scott Barrett, Vince Bartram and Eric Nixon – Mark Kendall did not have the greatest of debuts, conceding three goals in a disappointing defeat at Peterborough.

As a youngster, Kendall represented Tredegar and Gwent schools. He spent 15 months as an apprentice with Tottenham Hotspur before joining the professional ranks at White Hart Lane in July 1976. Nurtured along, he went on to appear in 36 senior matches for the London club as understudy to Barry Daines and Milija Aleksic, gaining his only Welsh Under-21 cap versus Scotland in February 1978, some 11 months before he made his Football League debut for Spurs against Norwich City. He had loan spells with both Chesterfield and Newport County before joining the latter club in November 1980 and gave the now defunct Somerton Park club tremendous service for over six years, playing in 317 first-class matches before transferring to Molineux for what was to prove a bargain fee of just £5,000.

At the time Wolves were struggling in 15th place in the old Fourth Division. Crowds were low – only 4,626 hardy supporters attended the previous home game against Exeter City on 27 December – but things were to improve.

With Kendall between the posts, progress was rapid. Wolves lost only three more League games that season, at home to Crewe Alexandra and away at Orient and Southend United, and qualified for the Play-offs after finishing fourth in the table. In fact, he and his stable defence gave away only 21 goals in 24 games during the second half of 1986–87, having conceded 29 in the first 20. Sadly in the end, after beating Colchester United over two legs, Wolves missed out on promotion, beaten by Aldershot 3–0 on aggregate in the Play-off Final.

Standing a fraction over 6ft tall and weighing 13st 9lb, Kendall was precisely the size and build for a great goalkeeper. He was strong in the air, had a safe pair of hands, was a good shot-stopper, commanded his area well and, above all, was brave and decisive in his actions. He was an ever present when Wolves doubled up by winning both the Fourth Division Championship and the Sherpa Van Trophy at Wembley in 1987–88, starring in a total of 61 senior games, his best overall return as a professional for one single campaign. Indeed, he was quite outstanding at times, producing brilliant displays in many crucial games. The following season (1988–89) he added a further 43 competitive appearances to his tally, helping Wolves clinch the Third Division title and reach the area Final of the Sherpa Van Trophy, beaten over two legs by Torquay United, although injury ruled him out of both of those two matches, loanee 'keeper Roger Hansbury taking over his duties.

Manager Turner recruited Tony Lange from Fulham as cover for Kendall in the summer of 1989, and he started the season as first choice, but Mark was soon back in favour, and he remained the club's number one until the end of the campaign when he was transferred to Swansea City for £25,000, Mike Stowell moving in to replace him.

There is no doubt that Kendall served Wolves extremely well. He had appeared in more than 175 competitive games and during his time at Molineux had reached the career milestone of 500 senior appearances, also topping the 450 mark in League football at the same time. He spent some 18 months at Vetch Field after leaving Molineux and while there had a loan spell with Burnley. After that he assisted Newport AFC, albeit only briefly, before joining the police force, based in Ebbw Vale. Still resident in South Wales, he is a member of the Wolves Former Players' Association, with several of his former teammates, and at one time his son, also a goalkeeper, was on the books of Crystal Palace.

PETER KNOWLES

Date of birth: 30 September 1945, Fitzwilliam near Frickley, Yorkshire

Wolves record:
Appearances: League 171+3, FA Cup 11, League 6
Goals: League 61, FA Cup 3, League Cup 0
Debut: League, 14 October 1963 v Leicester City (a) won 1–0

Also played for: Wath Wanderers, England (4 Under-23 caps)

The skilful Peter Knowles knew every trick in the book. Predominantly a goalscoring inside-forward, he also created opportunities for his colleagues with deft touches, clever flicks, reverse passes and neat headers, while regularly drawing defenders out of position with his excellent positional play and off-the-ball running.

Very effective in all aspects of forward play, Knowles, who gloried in a Wolves team playing two wingers and an out-and-out centre-forward, linked up splendidly with the former England international Ray Crawford in his first season in Wolves' League side (1963–64) and afterwards with Hugh McIlmoyle, Dave Woodfield (at times), then Derek Dougan and later Hugh Curran. He drew up a terrific understanding with the 'Doog', which started at the tail-end of the 1966–67 season as Wolves switched into top gear on their way to gaining promotion from the Second Division.

After signing as a professional at Molineux in October 1962 and accompanying the team on a successful tour to the US and Canada in May–June 1963, Knowles made his League debut at Filbert Street four months later and hit his first goal a week after that in a 2–2 home draw with Bolton.

Wolves had a disappointing 1964–65 season, which saw them relegated, but Knowles did well and established himself in the team, making 25 appearances in total. The following season (1965–66) he top scored with 21 goals (in League and FA Cup games), his haul including two cracking hat-tricks against Carlisle United (won 3–0) and Derby County (won 4–0), both in front of the Molineux supporters, most of whom certainly took him to their hearts, particularly the female element. He also scored a superb early goal at Southampton but this encounter turned out to be something of a nightmare as the Saints charged on to win 9–3.

In 1967–68 Knowles found the net 12 times as Wolves tried, successfully, to re-adjust to life back in the top flight. He had a brilliant game against Coventry City at Molineux, grabbing both goals in a 2–0 win, and he also starred in 3–2 and 6–1 home victories over Arsenal and Nottingham Forest respectively. Manager Ronnie Allen sincerely thought he was destined for full international honours, but unfortunately he didn't quite make it into Sir Alf Ramsey's squad, although he did play in four Under-23 matches against Wales and Italy in 1967–68 and Wales and Holland the following season, having earlier helped his country win the International Youth tournament in Holland, scoring in the Final against Spain.

In 1968–69 Knowles missed only three senior games out of a possible 47 and claimed another nine goals, producing a tremendous display in a 5–0 home win over Newcastle United. Bang in form at this time, he was now playing under a new manager Bill McGarry, who had stepped into the Molineux hot seat in October 1968. He began the 1969–70 campaign in style, scoring in each of the first three League matches in wins over Stoke City, Southampton and Sheffield Wednesday. But soon afterwards, at the age of 24, he rocked Molineux by announcing his retirement to pursue a new life as a Jehovah's Witness. His registration was retained by Wolves, who repeatedly asked him in vain to reconsider his decision.

So, unexpectedly, Peter Knowles said farewell to football, and no one could do anything about it.

It took quite a while for Wolves to find a suitable replacement in their forward line. Eventually Kenny Hibbitt was the man chosen.

A song by Billy Bragg – entitled *God's Footballer* – contained a commentary of one of Knowles's 64 goals he scored for Wolves in 191 appearances.

Peter, whose brother, the late Cyril Knowles, played for Tottenham Hotspur and managed Hartlepool United, is still working and living in the West Midlands.

JOLEON LESCOTT

Date of birth: 16 August 1982, Birmingham

Wolves record:
Appearances: League 205+6, FA Cup 10, League Cup 7+1, Others 5
Goals: League 13, FA Cup 0, League Cup 0, Others 0
Debut: League, 13 August 2000 v Sheffield Wednesday (h) drew 1–1

Joleon Lescott, who stands at 6ft 2in tall and weighs 13st, started out with the club's Centre of Excellence, joining the apprentice ranks in the summer of 1998 and turning professional in August 1999.

Lescott won honours for England at Under-18 level, and, after making his senior debut alongside the Frenchman Ludovic Pollet on the opening day of the 2000–01 campaign against Sheffield Wednesday in front of 19,000 fans at Molineux, he went on to have an excellent first season, making 37 League appearances. He also netted two goals – the first earned a point against Wimbledon in mid-September (1–1) and his second did likewise at home to Queen's Park Rangers on the very last day (also 1–1).

His mature displays belied his tender years, and for his noble efforts Lescott was voted Young Player of the Year by the Wolves supporters at the end of 2000–01. He maintained his form, produced many more outstanding performances and duly captured the same award for a second time the following season (2001–02) when he missed only two League games out of a possible 46 when forming a fine partnership at the back with Paul Butler, who had arrived from Sunderland halfway through the previous season.

As his game developed, Lescott became a lot fitter, looked much stronger, was more resilient and commanding at the heart of the Wolves defence and his superb displays earned him a call up to the England Under-20 squad for the International Youth Festival in Toulon in May 2002. As time progressed, he graduated to the England Under-21 set-up, winning two caps at this level (against Yugoslavia and Italy in 2003), while at the same time his displays in the gold and black of Wolves got increasingly better. He missed only one League game in 2002–03, starring in every match of the club's memorable FA Cup run, which ended in the sixth round at Southampton.

After helping Wolves claim their place in the Premiership for the first time by beating Sheffield United 3–0 in the First Division Play-off Final at the Millennium Stadium, Cardiff, in May 2003, Lescott underwent surgery to both of his knees – and unfortunately he didn't regain full fitness from these tedious operations in time to play in the top flight, being ruled out of the entire Premier League programme. He was gutted, but was confident that in years to come he would once more be part of a Wolves promotion-winning team! Despite that set-back and obvious disappointment at not being able to defend against the likes of Michael Owen and Alan Shearer, he was all geared up for the start of the 2004–05 First Division campaign. He played his first game in over a year during Wolves' pre-season summer tour of Norway and was then quickly back into his stride when League football resumed. He took no time at all to re-establish himself in the first team (as partner to Jody Craddock) and made 43 starts, scoring four goals, three of his strikes helping gain points against Sheffield United (3–3), Derby County (3–3) and Leicester City (1–1), all away from home. His other goal came in the home game against Sheffield United (won 4–2). His form earned him widespread acclaim, and after that he was as solid as a rock in the centre of Wolves' back four, receiving the senior Player of the Year award in 2005 after captaining the side. He signed a new two-and-a-half-year contract in October 2005, which would have kept him at Molineux until the summer of 2008, but he left in 2006 to join Everton for £5 million.

His elder brother Aaron (who was born in Birmingham in 1978) has played for Aston Villa, Sheffield Wednesday, Stockport County and Bristol Rovers.

WILF LOWTON

Date of birth: 3 October 1899, Exeter, Devon
Died: 12 January 1963, Exeter

Wolves record:
Appearances: League 198, FA Cup 11
Goals: League 25, FA Cup 2
Debut: League, 31 August 1929 v West Bromwich Albion (h) lost 4–2

Also played for: Heavitree United, Exeter City

Right full-back Wilf Lowton was one of the most powerful kickers of a dead ball in the game during the 1930s. He took all Wolves' penalties and free-kicks within shooting distance of the goal, and some of his enormous clearances, from a standing position with hardly any run up, often went sailing downfield first bounce into the goalkeeper's arms 100 yards away! This often annoyed his forwards, although occasionally he did set up a scoring opportunity, and he certainly put the opposing defence under pressure.

Captaining the side for several years, Lowton rendered yeoman service to Wolves, who signed him for just £1,400 from Exeter City prior to the start of the 1929–30 League campaign. He went straight into the first team in place of Len Williams and missed only two games that season, scoring two goals in successive home wins over Nottingham Forest and Bury, as Wolves finished ninth in the Second Division.

Lowton set off like a house on fire the following season, scoring a penalty in each of the opening three matches (all won) as Wolves set out their stall as one of the promotion favourites. Things were going along pretty well up to February, but after that, despite some battling performances by him and his co-defenders, the goals started to dry up, and as a result points were dropped at a fair rate of knots. In the end Wolves had to settle for fourth spot, missing promotion by a margin of 14 points.

Lowton, though, was optimistic, and in a message in the club's official programme early in the 1931–32 season he wrote 'The players, obviously disappointed at not gaining a place in the First Division, are confident of winning promotion this time. We are much stronger, and I know our forwards will score the goals, while the defenders, too, will be more determined than ever to keep the opposition at bay.' And so it proved. He had an outstanding season, sitting out only one game (the last against Charlton after suffering an injury the week before at Notts County) as Wolves, Leeds United and Stoke City battled it out for the two promotion places. In the end it was Wolves and Leeds who won through, Lowton's men taking the title by two points. He contributed nine goals from the penalty spot, two coming in a 7–1 win at Port Vale, and the team netted 115 goals to set a new record, and 71 of them were scored at Molineux, where Wolves lost only once.

Back in the top flight Lowton maintained his form, but the team struggled as a unit, just managing to avoid relegation thanks to a last match 4–2 home win over Everton. One of the tallest players in the side, he was now well into his 30s, yet he was still producing some great performances. He appeared in 38 of the 42 League games in 1933–34 as partner to Harry Shaw and, in fact, this duo was rated, in some quarters, as one of the best in top-flight football. At this juncture, however, manager Frank Buckley was ready to make changes to his team, and immediately he knew his days were numbered at Molineux.

Reg Hollingworth, fit after injury, was switched from centre-half to right-back at the start of the 1934–35 campaign and he did well. Lowton, as a reliable reserve, came in for just four more games (in November/December), and at the end of the season he returned to Exeter City, having accumulated a fine record with Wolves of 27 goals in 209 appearances. Now classed as a veteran, he made only 18 more appearances for the Grecians, finishing with an overall total of 97, having made his first in 1925 after previously playing for Ladysmith School (Exeter) and Heavitree United.

After retiring in May 1936, Lowton remained at St James's Park as a trainer for three months before illness forced him to give up. He lived in the Devon city until his death in January 1963, aged 63.

TOMMY LUNN

Date of birth:	9 July 1883, Bishop Auckland, County Durham
Died:	29 March 1960, Edmonton, North London

Wolves record:

Appearances:	League 129, FA Cup 13
Goals:	0
Debut:	League, 19 November 1904 v Preston North End (a) drew 2–2
Also played for:	Brownhills Albion, Tottenham Hotspur

Five months after gaining an FA Cup-winners' medal with Wolves, Tommy Lunn played in goal against Tottenham Hotspur in the first-ever League game staged at White Hart Lane on 1 September 1908. Then, in April 1910, he was transferred from Molineux to Spurs for £500.

Well-proportioned, strong and agile with a good positional sense, Lunn was not a giant. He stood at only 5ft 9in tall but challenging for balls with big, burly centre-forwards never seemed to worry him unduly. Always confident on his line, he took over between the posts for Wolves on a permanent basis from Tom Baddeley in March 1907, having acted as understudy to the England international for the previous two and a half years following his move to Molineux from Brownhills Albion in August 1904. He made 12 League appearances in his first season, when he conceded 29 goals; played in three League and two FA Cup matches in 1905–06 when he was beaten 12 times, five in a Cup replay at Bradford City, and had two more outings prior to making the number-one position his own with nine matches remaining in the 1906–07 campaign.

Tommy, who always wore a flat cap, regardless of the weather, produced some excellent displays during the next season when he was absent just four times as Wolves went all the way to the FA Cup Final, where they defeated Newcastle United 3–1 at Crystal Palace in front of almost 75,000 spectators.

A 'keeper who regularly punched the ball rather than collect it in his hands, Lunn retained his place throughout the next two seasons as Wolves battled without success to regain their First Division status, finishing seventh and eighth respectively. Then, with Cradley Heath-born Frank Boxley ready to replace him as first choice at Molineux, he was sold to Spurs by secretary-manager Jack Addenbrooke. He played in the last two League games for the London club that season and produced a superb display in the final one against Chelsea, which Spurs won 1–0 to stay in the First Division. He retained his place in the side for the next two seasons and starred for the Football League against the Southern League on his home patch at White Hart Lane in November 1910... his only representative honour.

Lunn was eventually replaced by John 'Tiny' Joyce, and, although reinstated for two games early in 1913, he went out and obtained a publican's licence, which was frowned upon by the Spurs' hierarchy and in breach of contract. Suspended as a consequence, he did not play again for the London club, and in June of that year he signed for Stockport County but appeared in only two competitive games for the Hatters before a serious leg injury forced him to retire.

Lunn returned to London after World War One and was nearing his 77th birthday when he died in 1960.

JOHN McALLE

Date of birth: Liverpool 31 January 1950

Wolves record:
Appearances: League 394+12, FA Cup 43+1, League Cup 27, European 18, Others 13
Goals: League 0, FA Cup 0, League Cup 1, European 2, Others 0
Debut: League, 29 April 1968 v Chelsea (a) lost 1–0

Also played for: Sheffield United, Derby County, Harrison's FC

Defender John McAlle signed for Wolves as an apprentice in July 1965 and turned professional 48 hours after his 17th birthday in February 1967. He spent the next three years playing mainly in the Central League side (the second XI) before establishing himself as a first-team regular in 1970, manager Bill McGarry engaging him at the heart of the defence alongside Frank Munro. He had been given his League baptism by previous boss Ronnie Allen in the away game at Chelsea in April 1968 when Wolves adopted a 5–3–2 system but had to wait until January 1969 for his next start (against Spurs in an FA Cup tie at White Hart Lane), although he did make a handful of substitute appearances in between times.

At the end of the 1970–71 season, McAlle collected a Texaco Cup-winners' medal (after the Scottish club Hearts had been beaten in the two-leg Final) while also taking his total number of senior appearances past the 60 mark. The following year, by which time he was playing exceptionally well, he scored his first goal for Wolves, but alas it was to no avail as Manchester City won a second-round League Cup tie 4–3 at Maine Road. And then, in May 1972, he played in the 1972 UEFA Cup Final against Spurs, having netted in both legs of the opening round encounter with the Portuguese side Academica Coimbra. Unfortunately for John, and Wolves, the London club proved too good overall and won the Final 3–2 on aggregate.

There was more disappointment for McAlle in 1972–73 when Wolves were beaten in two major semi-finals, losing to Leeds United 1–0 at Maine Road in the FA Cup and to their bogey side Spurs 4–3 on aggregate after two closely-fought contests in the League Cup.

In the First Division things weren't going too badly for Wolves, who finished fourth, ninth and fifth in that order between 1970 and 1973. Playing in a relatively settled team, McAlle's own form was very good, and in 1973–74 he missed only four out of a possible 57 games and collected his first major medal with the club. It came in the League Cup as Wolves overcame Manchester City 2–1 in the Wembley Final to lift the trophy for the first time.

Maintaining his form and his place over the next five seasons, McAlle had several different defensive partners, including Derek Jefferson, Mike Bailey (at times), Colin Brazier and Bob Hazell. Unfortunately Wolves were relegated after a horrible season in 1975–76, only to bounce straight back as Second Division champions under new manager Sammy Chung, McAlle collecting another winners' medal for his efforts in a solid defence that comprised Gary Pierce (in goal) Geoff Palmer and Derek Parkin at full-back and himself and Frank Munro in the centre.

After another FA Cup semi-final defeat, this time at the hands of Arsenal in March 1979, McAlle was replaced by new signing Emlyn Hughes from Liverpool, and with George Berry in the other defensive slot he became a regular reserve, getting few opportunities. However, he tragically broke his leg against Watford in a fifth-round FA Cup tie at Molineux in February 1980 and that ruled him out of contention for the rest of the season. In fact, he didn't return to first-team action for 11 months and, therefore, missed out on a second League Cup Final appearance as Wolves beat Nottingham Forest 1–0. He was never the same player after that mishap, and in August 1981 he joined Sheffield United for £10,000. He switched to Derby County two years later, and after leaving the Rams following relegation to the Third Division he moved into non-League football with Harrison's FC (Wolverhampton) while also working as a landscape gardener at the Merry Hill Shopping Centre, Brierley Hill, near Dudley before establishing his own landscape gardening business in Shropshire.

JIM McCALLIOG

Date of birth: Glasgow, 23 September 1946

Wolves record:
Appearances: League 158+5, FA Cup 9, League Cup 9+1, European 14, Others 14
Goals: League 34, FA Cup 4, League Cup 4, European 4, Others 2
Debut: League, 9 August 1969 v Stoke City (h) won 3–1

Also played for: Leeds United (amateur), Chelsea, Sheffield Wednesday, Manchester United, Southampton, Chicago Sting (NASL), Lynn Oslo (player-coach), Lincoln City (player-coach), Runcorn (player-manager), Scotland (2 Under-23 and 5 full caps)
Managed: Halifax Town

Jim McCalliog made his Football League debut for Chelsea at the age of 18 against arch-rivals Tottenham Hotspur and was one of the most expensive teenagers in football when he joined Sheffield Wednesday from Chelsea in 1965 for £37,500. It is interesting to know that when he joined Wednesday Jim's mother and father, three brothers and his sister all moved into the same house near Hillsborough. That's how closely-knit the McCalliog family was and, indeed, still is.

McCalliog became a top-class midfielder who represented Scotland in five full and two Under-23 internationals, having served his country at both Schoolboy and Youth-team levels as a teenager. An FA Cup finalist with the Owls in 1966 (beaten 3–2 by Everton), a decade later he celebrated in style when with Second Division underdogs Southampton as they beat his former employers Manchester United 1–0 in the Final, with him setting up the winning goal for Bobby Stokes. He had scored vital goals in previous rounds for the Saints in wins over Aston Villa and Bradford City.

McCalliog joined Wolves in July 1969, signed by Bill McGarry for £70,000. Linking up with Mike Bailey and Peter Knowles in midfield, he made an impressive home debut against Stoke City, setting up one of Derek Dougan's two goals in a 3–1 win. In his third game he netted against his former club Sheffield Wednesday, in a 3–2 victory at Hillsborough.

An excellent passer of the ball, McCalliog was an ever present in his first season with Wolves and missed only two League games the following season when he helped the Wanderers win the Texaco Cup, beating Heart of Midlothian 3–1 in the two-leg Final. Joined now in the engine room by Kenny Hibbitt, he was playing as well as ever and, in fact, reached double figures in the scoring charts for the first time in his career. His total of 10 included two in a 3–3 League draw at West Ham and a brace in a 5–1 FA Cup win over Norwich City.

Wolves had two excellent seasons in 1970–71 and 1971–72, finishing fourth and ninth respectively in the First Division table. They also reached the Final of the UEFA Cup in the second of those campaigns, McCalliog proving to be a vital member of the midfield trio along with skipper Mike Bailey and Hibbitt. He loved to swing passes out to his winger Dave Wagstaffe and proved to be very effective on the European scene. He produced brilliant performances against the Dutch side Den Haag in round two, Juventus in the quarter-final and Ferencvaros of Hungary in the semis. He also played well in the two-leg Final against Tottenham Hotspur, scoring in the first leg at Molineux, which Wolves lost 2–1. Unfortunately, despite a plucky away display which saw him strike the outside of a post, Wolves could only draw in the return leg 1–1 and as a result missed out on another trophy, losing 3–2 on aggregate.

Injuries affected McCalliog's performances during the 1972–73 season and again throughout the first part of the following campaign. This certainly annoyed him, and perhaps it came as a surprise to the supporters when he was transferred to Manchester United for £60,000, a few days after Wolves had beaten Manchester City 2–1 in the League Cup Final, which he missed, having lost his place in the side to Alan Sunderland.

The recipient of a Second Division Championship-winners' medal with Manchester United in 1974–75, McCalliog left Old Trafford for Southampton in a £45,000 deal in February 1975. After a spell in the NASL and in Norway, he also served Lincoln City as player-coach in 1978–79, acting as caretaker manager for a while before Colin Murphy was appointed.

After being released in March 1979, McCalliog dropped into non-League football with Runcorn, combining his role as player-manager with that of football in the community officer at Blackburn, later fulfilling the same role at Halifax Town, whom he also managed. After scouting for Leyton Orient, he worked as a journalist before becoming a licensee, running the George & Dragon pub in Wetherby and later the County Hotel in Harrogate.

During his nomadic career McCalliog amassed over 550 club appearances. One of his brothers, Fred, was on Sheffield Wednesday's books for a short time.

BOBBY MASON

Date of birth: 22 March 1936, Tipton, Staffordshire

Wolves record:
Appearances: League 146, FA Cup 14, European 11, Others 2
Goals: League 44, FA Cup 5, European 5, Others 0
Debut: League, 5 November 1955 v Luton Town (a) lost 5–1

Also played for: Chelmsford City, Leyton Orient, Poole Town

Inside-forward Bobby Mason spent 11 years at Molineux and was a regular member of the first team between November 1957 and November 1961. He joined the club as an amateur in July 1951 and turned professional two months after his 18th birthday.

With so many talented goalscoring inside and centre-forwards at the club around this time, including Peter Broadbent, Roy Swinbourne and Dennis Wilshaw, Mason was nurtured along in the reserves and, in fact, he scored plenty of goals at this level, helping Wolves' second XI win the Central League title in 1952–53, gaining a second winners' medal in 1957–58, the same season he established himself in the first XI.

Blessed with a sturdy little frame, Mason was one of the nearest things to perpetual motion one could find in top-flight football in the later 1950s to early 1960s. Fired by tremendous determination, he gave nothing less than 100 percent on the field of play and often received high praise from his manager Stan Cullis for some superb performances. 'There is no substitute for hard work' was the stark message that hung on the home dressing room wall at Molineux when he was in his prime, and he certainly produced the goods week in, week out, with some superb displays as Wolves won successive League championships in 1957–58 and 1958–59. He was a vital part of the team's attacking set-up, and when interviewed some years after leaving Molineux he clearly remembered that message, revealing that those seven words, without doubt, made him into the player he was. He acknowledged the advice given to him by the senior and more experienced players at the club, which proved invaluable as he continued to improve his game.

Mason made his League debut at inside-right against newly-promoted Luton Town in a First Division match at Kenilworth Road on 5 November 1955, but it was the Hatters who produced the fireworks, winning 5–1. He recalled 'It was an unhappy day, not only for me but also for Roy Swinbourne who was badly injured and retired two years later.' At this juncture, he was on the verge of becoming a permanent fixture in Wolves' forward line. He had made a further nine senior appearances in 1956–57 and had netted his first goal in a 4–3 home League win over Preston North End. Jimmy Murray had come in to replace Swinbourne as leader of the attack, with Broadbent and Wilshaw occupying the two inside berths. However, Wilshaw was injured in the local derby against West Bromwich Albion, and Mason took over his position, scoring immediately in a 4–3 win at Manchester City. He held his place, and when Wilshaw was transferred to Stoke City shortly before Christmas he knew that if he could maintain his form and work hard at his game he would make the inside-left position his own. He did just that, and at the end of the season he duly collected his first senior medal as Wolves won the League title for the second time in their history.

The following season, Mason, who was switched to inside-right halfway through the campaign, missed eight League games but netted 13 goals, including his first hat-trick in an 5–1 opening day League win over Nottingham Forest. He also played in Wolves' first-ever European Cup game against Schalke 04. Full of confidence, he started 1959–60 by scoring the winning goal against Birmingham City. He continued to perform well and netted four goals in the European Cup competition and two in a fifth-round FA Cup win over Luton as Wolves surged on towards Wembley. Sadly, he never made the Final, being replaced by Barry Stobart.

Putting that disappointment behind him, Mason remained loyal to Wolves for another two years before joining Chelmsford City, after spells with Leyton Orient and Poole Town. He retired in 1965, at which point he returned to the Midlands, later residing in Christchurch (Dorset) and Swadlincote.

WWFC
FC

KENNY MILLER

Date of Birth: 23 December 1979, Edinburgh

Wolves record:
Appearances: League 134+38, FA Cup 10+2, League Cup 6+1, Others 3+2
Goals: League 53, FA Cup 5, League Cup 5, Others 0
Debut: League, 8 September 2001 v Preston North End (a) won 2–1

Also played for: Stenhousemuir, Hibernian, Rangers, Celtic, Scotland (1 B, 7 Under-21, 22 full caps)

Kenny Miller was an instant hit with the Molineux fans after joining Wolves on a three-month loan deal from Glasgow Rangers in September 2001. He was subsequently signed on a permanent basis for £3 million when his loan spell ended in mid-December.

Miller began his career with Hibernian, for whom he signed as a professional in 1997. He had a loan spell with Stenhousemuir halfway through the 1997–98 season, when he scored eight times in 11 outings. Returning to Easter Road full of confidence, he went on to net 14 goals in a total of 53 appearances for Hibs, who then sold him to the Glasgow Rangers for £2 million in July 2000, after he agreed to a five-year contract (which never matured).

Miller did well with the 'Gers, claiming an overall tally of 11 goals (including a record 5 against St Mirren in 2000) in 39 matches before teaming up with Wolves on a permanent basis. A former Scottish Young Player of the Year, his first two appearances for Wolves were both as a substitute against Preston North End and Stockport County. In his first start at Gillingham, he scored in front of the travelling supporters to celebrate the occasion as Wolves won 3–2, courtesy of a last-minute goal from Shaun Newton. He was on target again three days later in a 3–0 win at Walsall, but in his fifth match he fell awkwardly after going up for a header during the game with Nottingham Forest and suffered a fractured a collar bone. This kept him out of action for six weeks.

Miller was scheduled to return to Ibrox Park just before Christmas 2001, but manager Dave Jones successfully negotiated a deal with his counterpart at Rangers (Alex McLeish, ex-Hibs, who had just taken over at Ibrox) and secured his services on a permanent basis, to the delight of the supporters, who by this time had taken him to their hearts. He signed a four-and-a-half-year contract at Molineux, but there were three other business-like strikers at the club at the time – Dean Sturridge, Adam Proudlock and Nathan Blake – and in his first season he made only 5 full appearances and 15 as a substitute.

However, a pre-season injury kept Sturridge out of the opening games at the start of 2002–03, gifting Miller a chance to stake a claim. The young Scot grasped the opportunity with both hands, although he made a rather slow start before eventually overtaking Nathan Blake's goal tally to become the season's leading scorer. By the end of the term his total in League and Cup competitions stood at 24, one of the most precious being his effort in the Play-off Final victory over Sheffield United in May 2003.

In the Premiership, Miller enjoyed mixed fortunes scoring just twice in 25 outings (eight as a substitute), but he did have the pleasure of cracking home the only goal of the game when Wolves beat Manchester United at Molineux in mid-January.

With Wolves heading back to the First Division, Miller slipped out of favour, Carl Cort taking over the main striker's role, but the Scot stuck in there, and despite handing in a transfer request in the summer of 2004 he remained at Molineux. It was lucky he did. Injuries meant that he went straight into the starting line up for 2004–05 and went on to form a very useful partnership with Cort, Miller ending up as top scorer with 20 goals to his credit, while Cort netted 16. A hamstring injury sustained in October 2005 confined him to the treatment room, but he battled hard to regain his fitness and returned to action before the end of the year, only to sign a pre-contract agreement with Celtic in January 2006. He moved to Parkhead officially the following June after scoring 64 goals in just under 200 senior games for Wolves.

BILL MORRIS

Date of birth: 26 March 1913, Handsworth, Birmingham
Died: 1995, Dudley

Wolves record:
Appearances: League 175, FA Cup 22, Wartime 67
Goals: League 2, FA Cup 1, Wartime 1
Debut: League, 17 February 1934 v West Bromwich Albion (a) lost 0-2

Also played for: Handsworth Old Boys, West Bromwich Albion (amateur), Halesowen Town, Wrexham (guest), Dudley Town, England (3 caps)

Intrinsically a natural footballer, Bill Morris was able to play, and play well, in almost any outfield position, but preferred to defend rather than attack. After appearing in all three half-back berths and as an inside-forward, he started his senior career as a centre-half in West Brom's colts side. He occupied several positions with Halesowen before settling down at centre-half for Wolves, a position he retained until Stan Cullis arrived on the scene in the mid 1930s. Bill was then switched to right-back by manager Frank Buckley, where he became a grand mobile performer and in which position he earned three full caps for England, all in 1938–39, against Ireland (won 7–0), Scotland (2–1) and Romania (2–0), as well as appearing in that season's FA Cup Final defeat by Portsmouth at Wembley.

Signed for just £100 in May 1933, Morris, who was a strong kicker and tackler, mobile with great positional sense, actually made his Football League debut as an emergency centre-forward against his former club West Bromwich Albion in February 1934. With both Billy Hartill and George Goddard out injured, he was asked to partner another reserve, Irvine Harwood, in attack as the Baggies won 2–0.

The following season Wolves' more senior half-backs were Dicky Rhodes, Tom Smalley, Jack Nelson and Dai Richards, with Morris acting as reserve to all four. He was given eight senior outings, six in succession in place of Smalley at centre-half during March and April. Then, at the start of the 1935–36 campaign, he became first-choice pivot, and he performed superbly well alongside Smalley, Rhodes and Richards and also with Joe Gardiner and Tom Galley. He also found time to score his first senior goal to earn a point from a 2–2 draw at Chelsea, quickly following up with a second strike in a 3–1 FA Cup replay defeat at Leeds.

Wolves struggled at the start of 1936–37, losing five of their opening nine League games. This prompted manager Buckley to switch Morris to right-back and install Stan Cullis at centre-half. Both players never looked back, and Morris went on to become one of the best full-backs in the country.

World War Two obviously disrupted Morris's career as it did many others footballers. He appeared in almost 70 regional games for Wolves as well as guesting for Wrexham, and he had the pleasure of scoring the winning goal in the longest game in Wolves' history – in the 153rd minute of a League Cup North encounter against Birmingham in 1945. When peacetime football resumed in 1946, he knew it was going to be hard to retain his place in the side. He started the first League season after the hostilities in the right-back position as partner to Gus Mclean, but after 10 games he lost his place when new manager Ted Vizard switched McLean to the right and introduced Billy Crook on the left flank.

Morris, who was now 33, remained at Molineux until the end of that campaign when he joined nearby Dudley Town, spending two seasons in the Birmingham League playing as a centre-forward before retiring in May 1949. He was 82 when he died in 1995.

JIMMY MULLEN

Date of birth: 6 January 1923, Newcastle-upon-Tyne
Died: October 1987, Wolverhampton

Wolves record:
Appearances: League 445, FA Cup 98, Others 3, Wartime 88
Goals: League 98, FA Cup 14, Others 0, Wartime 27
Debut: League, 18 February 1939 v Leeds United (h) won 4–1

Also played for: England (12 caps)

One of the most talented footballers of his generation, Jimmy Mullen thrilled the crowds at Molineux in a career that spanned 20 years. Learning his soccer with St Mary's Junior and St Aloysius Roman Catholic Schools, he represented both Newcastle and Northumberland Boys and was a regular supporter at St James' Park.

Mullen could have joined his home-town club but one of his teachers advised him of the excellent youth policy at Molineux and that potentially Wolves was a better club! So the young Geordie moved to Wolverhampton in June 1937, shortly after playing for England in a Schoolboy international. Under the shrewd guidance of his manager Major Buckley, he developed fast and made his first-team debut in February 1939 at the age of 16. Occupying the outside-right position, he started well, crossing for Dennis Westcott to head home a fifth-minute goal in a 4–1 win. He appeared in a further seven League and two FA Cup games that season. His second Cup outing was the semi-final clash with Grimsby Town when a record Old Trafford crowd of 76,962 saw Wolves thrash the Mariners by 5–0. Unfortunately he didn't make the Final team, which Wolves surprisingly lost to Portsmouth.

Signing professional forms in 1940, Mullen played as a guest for Darlington and Leicester City during the early part of the war (his colleague Billy Wright was with him at Filbert Street). He then served as a soldier in the Army from 1942, based at Farnborough, Catterick and Barnard Castle (Durham). After scoring 27 goals in 88 games for Wolves during the hostilities, in the first peacetime League season of 1946–47 he only missed four games and netted 11 times.

Having gained three England caps in wartime football, against Wales (twice) and Belgium, Mullen made his senior debut against Scotland at Wembley in April 1947. He was all set to face France soon afterwards, but Wolves withdrew him, stating that he was required for a vital League game against Portsmouth instead. It was to be another two years before he appeared for England again.

Fast moving and clever on the ball, Mullen loved to cut inside his full-back and have a crack at goal, and he was a terrific crosser of the ball as well. A member of the Wolves side that beat Leicester City 3–1 in the 1949 FA Cup Final, he added further caps to his tally against Norway and France that same year, while in May 1950 he became England's first ever substitute against Belgium at the Heysel Stadium. He also played in two 1950 World Cup games against Chile (won) and the USA (lost), the latter being that disastrous 1–0 reverse in Belo Horizonte.

Back on the domestic front, Mullen netted seven times in 38 games when Wolves won their first League title in 1953–54. He also won six more caps that same season, his 12th and last coming against Switzerland in the World Cup Finals.

Mullen participated in some of the famous floodlit matches of the 1950s and won two more League Championship medals in 1957–58 and 1958–59, making his final appearance for Wolves against Spurs at Molineux in March 1959. He remained at the club for another season before announcing his retirement in May 1960 – just after Wolves had won the FA Cup.

Granted a testimonial by the club in 1962 (which he shared with Billy Wright), Mullen later ran a successful sports shop in the town until 1987. Sadly, just a year later, he died, leaving the town of Wolverhampton and football in general, mourning a truly great player who was affectionately known as 'Gentleman Jim' both on and off the pitch.

WEMBLEY 1974

FRANK MUNRO

Date of birth:	25 October 1947, Dundee, Scotland
Wolves record:	
Appearances:	League 290+6, FA Cup 20, League Cup 23, European 17, Others 15
Goals:	League 14, FA Cup 0, League Cup 2, European 3, Others 0
Debut:	League, 13 January 1968 v Leicester City (a) lost 3–1
Also played for:	Chelsea (groundstaff), Dundee United, Aberdeen, Celtic, Hellas (Australia), Scotland (9 full and 4 Under-23 caps)

In the summer of 1967, shortly after regaining their First Division status, Wolves, masquerading as 'Los Angeles Wolves', took part in (and won) a North American international soccer tournament, organised by a Canadian millionaire. In the Final they defeated Aberdeen 6–5 after extra-time, and playing at the heart of the Dons' defence was Frank Munro, who bagged a hat-trick including two penalties. Impressed with what he saw from the 19-year-old Scot from Broughty Ferry, manager Ronnie Allen immediately opened negotiations with the Pittodrie Park club, and six months later, in January 1968, he succeeded in signing him for what proved to be a bargain fee of just £55,000.

Munro, who was on Chelsea's groundstaff as a 15-year-old, started his League career in earnest with Dundee United and gained four Youth caps and played in two amateur internationals for his country before turning professional in July 1963. He had appeared in only 60 first-team games for Aberdeen, gaining a Scottish Cup runners'-up medal in 1967. He was highly-rated at Pittodrie Park by boss Eddie Turnbull and, indeed, was already in line to become Scotland's next centre-half.

Big and burly and a real bulwark yet very skilled, Munro was terrific in the air, possessed a biting tackle and revealed ball control mostly associated with a craftsman inside-forward. He made his debut, alongside Dave Woodfield, in the centre of the Wolves defence against Leicester City a few days after moving to Molineux. However, he had to wait until August 1969 before gaining a regular place in the side, teaming up this time with John Holsgrove. At this juncture, Bill McGarry was now in charge at Molineux, and he thought Munro was one of the First Division's most outstanding central-defenders, often praising him for some tremendous displays.

Unfortunately Munro was banned for a month during the 1969–70 season (for receiving far too many cautions) and as a result missed several games, but he came back with a vengeance, showing great tenacity and commitment and helping Wolves win the Texaco Cup in May 1971. Later in the month he gained the first two of his nine full caps for Scotland, coming on as a second-half substitute against Northern Ireland at Hampden Park and England at Wembley. His other seven appearances were made against Denmark and USSR in June 1971 and versus Sweden, Wales, Northern Ireland, England and Romania during 1974–75. Frank was also capped four times at Under-23 level (1969–71).

In May 1972, having produced some very impressive displays, Munro was bitterly disappointed when Wolves were defeated by Tottenham Hotspur in the UEFA Cup Final. The following year he cursed his luck again as Wolves lost two major semi-finals, going down to Leeds United in the FA Cup and Spurs in the League Cup. All was to change, however, in March 1974 when he and his Wolves colleagues won the League Cup for the very first time, beating Manchester City 2–1 before a crowd of almost 98,000 at Wembley. Retaining his place in the side for the next three seasons, he amassed a total of 371 senior appearances for Wolves. He eventually left the club in May 1977, following a change of manager (Sammy Chung having replaced McGarry) and relegation to the Second Division. He returned to Scotland and signed for Celtic for £20,000, playing in the 1978 Scottish Cup Final defeat by Rangers.

After leaving Parkhead, Munro had a brief spell with the strong Australian club Hellas before holding coaching positions with Albion Rovers and later with Hamlyn Rangers and Keilor FC in Austria. After returning to England, Frank suffered the first of two strokes in 1993. A member of the former Wolves Former Players' Association, he is currently living in the West Midlands and regularly attends games at Molineux.

JIMMY MURRAY

Date of birth: 11 October 1935, Dover

Wolves record:
Appearances: League 273, FA Cup 14, Europe 9, Others 3
Goals: League 155, FA Cup 7, Europe 2, Others 2
Debut: League, 12 November 1955 v Charlton Athletic (h) won 2–0.

Also played for: Manchester City, Walsall, Telford United, England (2 Under-23 caps)

Wolves manager Stan Cullis always believed that Jimmy Murray would become a top-class goalscorer, and so it proved. Having joined the Molineux club as a youngster – spotted by George Poyser, the same scout who found Peter Broadbent – Jimmy was doing his National Service at Lichfield when, just 24 hours before Wolves' home friendly against Moscow Dynamo in early November 1955, he picked up a local newspaper and saw the headline 'Unknown to lead Wolves'. The 19-year-old was staggered, but it was true, and soon afterwards he received a telephone call from his boss confirming that he was to replace the injured Roy Swinbourne under the Molineux floodlights. He acquitted himself well and helped Wolves to a fine 2–1 win in front of more than 55,000 fans.

Murray never looked back after that introduction and went on to become an excellent marksman, partnering Dennis Wilshaw and then Bobby Mason as the main strike force for Wolves' front line. Despite being only 5ft 9in tall, he was razor-sharp inside the penalty-area and had the knack of being in the right place at the right time. He scored some stunning goals and was leading marksman in League action in both of Wolves' First Division Championship-winning campaigns of 1957–58 and 1958–59, notching 29 and 21 respectively. He again topped the charts in 1959–60 with 33 goals as Wolves won the FA Cup.

Murray established himself in Wolves' first team during the 1955–56 season, scoring 11 times in 25 League games. The following term he netted a further 17 goals in 33 starts, four coming on the opening Saturday when Manchester City were hammered 5–1 at Molineux. With the goals flowing thick and fast from a rampant Wolves side, he recorded two superb hat-tricks in 1957–58 against Birmingham City and Nottingham Forest, and he netted in each of the last seven League games of 1958–59, two of them proving to be vital winners at Blackpool and Everton. His efforts earned him two England Under-23 caps against Scotland and France.

Ted Farmer joined Murray in the Wolves attack in 1960–61, and between them they claimed 53 goals, Jimmy notching 25 before contributing another 17 in 1961–62 and eight the following term to bring his final total in a Wolves shirt to an impressive 166 in 299 senior appearances, and his exquisite scoring exploits weren't simply confined to the first XI. He bagged almost 100 further goals in reserve and youth-team football, cracking in a double hat-trick in a Central League match against Chesterfield in 1961.

When Murray eventually left Molineux for Manchester City in a £27,000 deal in November 1963, only two players had scored more goals for Wolves at first-team level – Billy Hartill with 194 and Johnny Hancocks with 168 – and he is one of only four players to have netted over 150 in League football for the club.

Murray made an immediate impact at Maine Road, hitting 12 goals in his first six matches, forming a terrific partnership in attack with Derek Kevan, the former West Bromwich Albion and England centre-forward. He later contributed seven important goals in the first half of City's Second Division Championship-winning season of 1965–66, and he continued to score consistently after that, first for Walsall and then for Telford United, whom he helped reach two consecutive FA Trophy Finals before retiring in 1971.

After retiring from football, Murray ran a successful greengrocery business in Tamworth before working for a contract car hire company. He currently lives in Lichfield.

MANDERS
PAINT & INK

ANDY MUTCH

Date of birth: 28 December 1963, Liverpool.

Wolves record:
Appearances: League 227+12, FA Cup 11+1, League Cup 14, Others 23
Goals: League 96, FA Cup 2, League Cup 4, Others 4
Debut: League, 8 March 1986 v Rotherham United (h) drew 0–0

Also played for: Everton, Liverpool, Southport, Swindon Town, Wigan Athletic, Stockport County, Barrow, Telford United, England (3 B caps)

Plucked out of non-League obscurity by Wolves manager Sammy Chapman in 1986, Andy Mutch went on to form a terrific strike partnership with Steve Bull. They were at the club together for a period of seven and a half years, during which time they netted 301 goals, Andy's contribution being 84, 'Bully's' 217.

An apprentice with both Merseyside clubs, Everton and Liverpool, Mutch spent two seasons with Southport before arriving at Molineux when Wolves were battling (in vain) to avoid relegation to the Fourth Division. He scored seven goals in 15 games at the end of that 1985–86 campaign, the first in a 2–1 home League win over Bristol City a week before Easter.

Mutch netted seven times at the start of the following campaign before he was joined in attack by Bull. Virtually straightaway their partnership bore fruit, and when the season ended they had bagged 35 goals between them, but alas their efforts on this occasion weren't enough to earn Wolves promotion as they missed out in the Play-offs.

Twelve months on and things were much more rosy at Molineux after Wolves had doubled up by winning the Fourth Division Championship and the Sherpa Van Trophy. Mutch, an ever present that season, weighed in with 23 goals (19 in the League), and he also had the pleasure of netting at Wembley when Burnley were defeated 2–0 in the Final of the SVT before a crowd of 80,841 – the largest audience he ever played in front of as a professional footballer.

In the summer of 1989 – after his 21 goals had helped Wolves win the Third Division title – Mutch was rewarded for his efforts on the field, with three England B caps against Switzerland, Norway and Iceland. He started every game, the first two with Bull as his strike partner, and they were together at the end of the final match as well. Among the other players who starred in these games were Paul Gascoigne, Gary Pallister, David Platt, Gary Mabbutt and Tony Dorigo.

Back to the bread and butter of League and Cup football, Mutch continued where he had left off by claiming 12 goals in 1989–90, but he was now finding it a lot harder at a higher level of football and mustered only eight in 1990–91 and 10 the following season (including a hat-trick in a 6–2 home League win over Newcastle United) before bowing out with another 10 in 1992–93 as Wolves struggled to make headway towards the Play-offs. His last goal in a Wolves shirt earned his team a 1–0 home win over Newcastle United in April 1993.

Mutch left Molineux with his head held high, having scored on average a goal every three games while laying on loads more for 'Bully' and his fellow teammates. An unselfish forward, quick off the mark with a good first touch, he was excellent in the air and had the knack of knowing where 'Bully' was or would be once he headed the ball on or fed it into a space. Signed by Swindon Town for £250,000 in the summer of 1993, he spent one season in the Premiership with the Robins and later had a loan spell with Wigan Athletic (August 1995) before joining Stockport County in April 1996. After helping the Hatters win promotion to the First Division in 1997, he returned to the Conference League with Barrow before rejoining his former club Southport in January 1999. He was later engaged as player and assistant manager by Telford United (1999–2000).

Mutch is currently a member of the Wolves former Players' Association, and he is living in Lancashire.

GEOFF PALMER

Date of birth:	11 July 1954, Cannock, Staffordshire
Wolves record:	
Appearances:	League 410+6, FA Cup 38, League Cup 33, European 6, Others 2
Goals:	League 13, FA Cup 1, League Cup 2, European 0, Others 0
Debut:	League, 13 October 1973 v Birmingham City (a) lost 2–1
Also played for:	Burnley, Staffordshire Police, England (2 Under-23 caps)

Uncompromising full-back Geoff Palmer had two spells with Wolves, and in all he spent 16 years at Molineux, amassing almost 500 senior appearances, making him one of the finest servants the club has ever had. A sterling performer, full of energy and commitment, he had plenty of skill which complemented a fine physique. A strong kicker of the ball from any angle, he was able to contain the trickiest of wingers and all in all was a solid defender, confident in his own ability.

Twice a League Cup winner with Wolves – in 1974 versus Manchester City and 1980 versus Nottingham Forest – Palmer twice helped the team gain promotion from the old Second Division in 1977 (as champions) and 1983 (as runners-up) and played in all four Divisions of the Football League (before the Premiership was introduced in 1992). He also gained two England Under-23 caps against Wales and Portugal in the mid 1970s.

Palmer joined Wolves as an apprentice in July 1970 and turned professional 12 months later on his 17th birthday. Reserve to Bernard Shaw, Derek Parkin and Gerry Taylor for two seasons, he made his League debut in place of Taylor in the Midlands derby with Birmingham City at St Andrew's 11 games into the 1973–74 season and never really looked back after that. He scored his first goal at senior level in a 3–1 win at Tottenham Hotspur six weeks after his introduction to first-class soccer and celebrated in style with his colleagues some four months later when the League Cup was won at Wembley.

Injuries and suspensions interrupted both the 1974–75 and 1975–76 campaigns, but in 1976–77, as an ever present, Palmer performed admirably as Wolves won the Second Division title at the first attempt following relegation 12 months earlier. Firmly establishing himself as Derek Parkin's full-back partner, he continued to perform consistently well, but, along with his colleagues, he was bitterly disappointed when Wolves lost to Arsenal in the semi-final of the FA Cup at Villa Park in 1979. However, a year on he was over the moon as Wolves again lifted the League Cup at Wembley, only for the team to slip up once more in another FA Cup semi-final 12 months later, losing this time to Arsenal's North London rivals Tottenham.

Season 1981–82 proved to be a disaster for Wolves as they crashed through the First Division's trapdoor for the second time in six years, but the team responded greatly to the challenge and regained top-flight status at the first attempt, Palmer contributing five goals, including crucial ones in wins over Derby County (h) and Burnley (a) and the draw at Shrewsbury. Unfortunately Wolves could not cope with the Liverpools, Manchester Uniteds, Arsenals and so forth and slipped back into the Second Division in 1984. At this juncture, with Tommy Docherty in charge, his position in the side came under pressure. It resulted in him leaving for Burnley in November of that year, only for him to rejoin the club 13 months later, re-signed by his former boss Bill McGarry who had returned to the club a month earlier. By this time Wolves were in the Third Division and it got no better as Geoff went down with his teammates to Division Four at the end of the 1985–86 campaign. He played just once at this level before retiring to join the police force (initially based in Cannock). He played for the police team in the Midland Combination and later assisted ex-Wolves star Steve Daley as coach of Bromsgrove Rovers (1998–99).

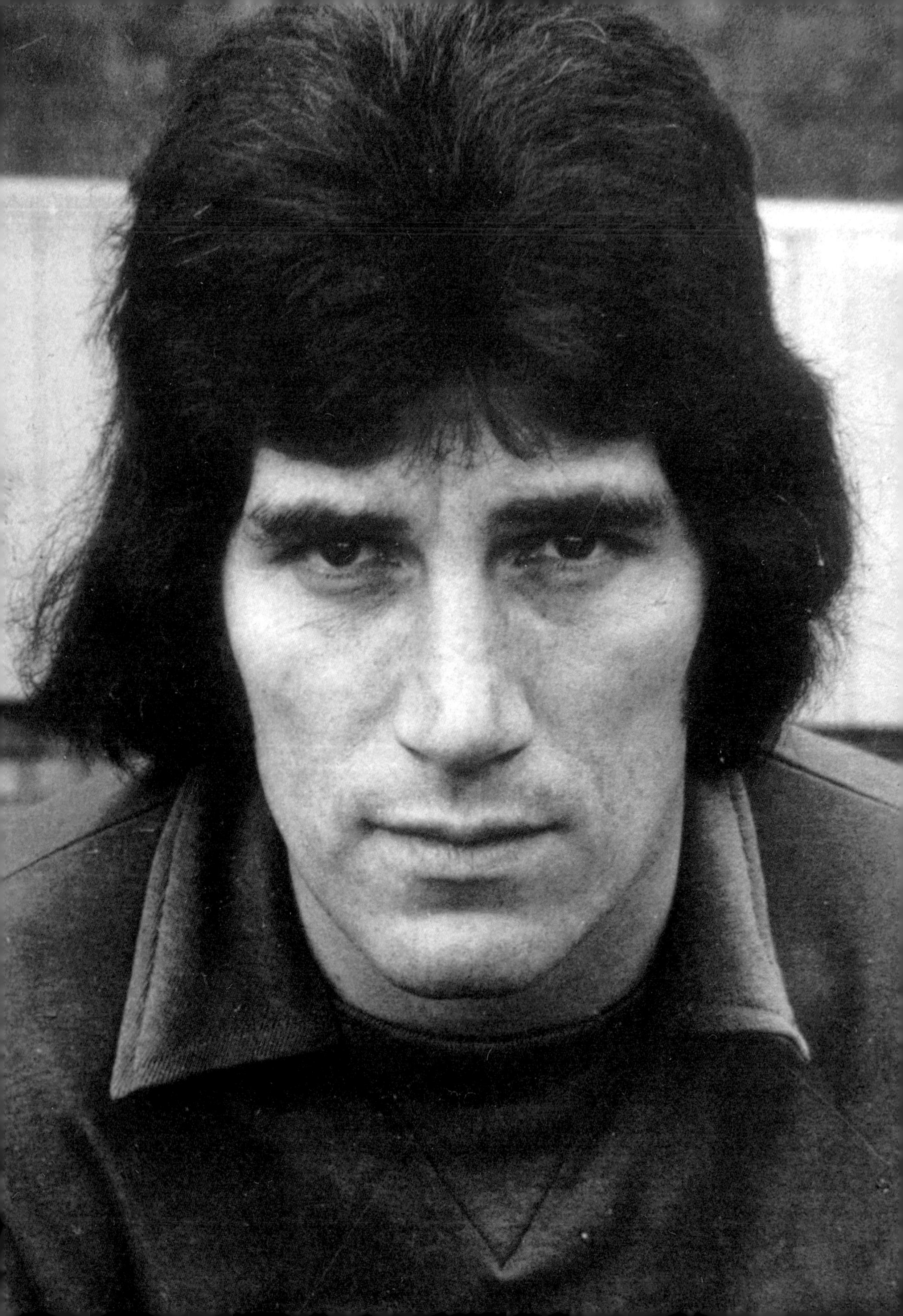

PHIL PARKES

Date of birth:	14 July 1947, West Bromwich
Wolves record:	
Appearances:	League 303, FA Cup 23, League Cup 23, European 16, Others 17
Goals:	0
Debut:	League, 19 November 1967 v Preston North End (h) won 3–2
Also played for:	Vancouver Whitecaps, Chicago Sting, Toronto Blizzard, San Jose Earthquakes (All NASL), Marstons FC

Goalkeeper Phil 'Lofty' Parkes, 6ft 4in tall, supported West Bromwich Albion as a lad and actually attended the local grammar school and represented the town's football team. He joined Wolves as an apprentice in August 1962 and turned professional just as manager Stan Cullis was about to leave Molineux in September 1964.

With Fred Davies and Dave MacLaren sharing the number-one spot, Parkes was confined to Central League football over the next two years before making his senior debut against Preston North End in November 1966, when Davies was sidelined through injury. He made a terrific start to his League career, saving a penalty in a 3–2 win as Wolves continued their promotion battle with Coventry City at the top of the Second Division table. He made 14 appearances that season, helping Wolves regain their top-flight status after a break of just two years. They finished second, a point behind the Sky Blues, after losing their last game at Crystal Palace when a draw would have given them the title.

Parkes was first choice when the 1967–68 season got under way at Fulham, Wolves winning 2–1. He played in his first-ever Black Country derby at home to Albion four days later, but he had the misfortune to get sent off in a 3–3 draw watched by almost 52,500 spectators. He missed a third of the games that season, Evan Williams and Davies pushing him all the way. A third goalkeeper, Alan Boswell, then arrived on the scene, but Phil maintained his form and his position as Wolves further consolidated their place in Division One. Manager Ronnie Allen was replaced by Bill McGarry in 1968, but he still held his place by producing some excellent displays while taking his overall appearance tally past the 100 mark before the end of 1970–71 after Wolves had won the Texaco Cup (against Hearts).

Parkes had his best season (up to that point of his career) in 1971–72. An ever present, playing in all 57 competitive games, he conceded only 74 goals as Wolves reached the UEFA Cup Final where, disappointingly, they lost over two legs to Tottenham Hotspur. The following season when, for the second time running, he played in every first-class match (59), he was in sight of two Wembley Finals but in the end didn't make either of them, Wolves losing to their, by now, bogey side Spurs 4–3 on aggregate in the semi-final of the League Cup and going down 1–0 to Leeds United in the semi-final of the FA Cup.

In June 1973 manager McGarry recruited Gary Pierce from Huddersfield Town to put pressure on Parkes, who took the challenge in his stride, although the presence of a new 'keeper resulted in him missing out on a first Wembley appearance. He played in the opening six League games of the 1973–74 campaign and had created a new club record when Pierce replaced him for the away clash at Newcastle in mid-September – bringing to an end a run of 127 consecutive League appearances (from 1 September 1970) and 171 in all competitions . It was tit for tat for the number-one position as the games rolled by, and when it came to the crunch match – the League Cup Final against Manchester City at Wembley in March 1974 – the luckless Phil, who had played in all the previous rounds, missed out through injury. Three years later he never got a game as Wolves won the Second Division title, Pierce once more being regarded as first choice.

Parkes, who effectively retired from League football after his testimonial match in 1978, also assisted four clubs in the NASL over a period of two years, winning the Super Bowl with Vancouver Whitecaps in 1979 when he had Bruce Grobbelaar to contend with. He also played for non-League side Marstons, managed a handful of other local clubs, turned out for the Wolves Old Stars in charity matches and had a spell as coach at Bromsgrove Rovers when ex-Wolves midfielder Steve Daley was boss there. In 2006 he was recruited by his former Wolves playing colleague Mel Eves as goalkeeping coach at Willenhall Town.

He also played cricket for Fordhouses in the Wolverhampton League. Only Mike Stowell and Bert Williams have made more appearances in goal for Wolves than Phil 'Lofty' Parkes.

DEREK PARKIN

Date of birth: 2 January 1946, Newcastle-upon-Tyne

Wolves record:
Appearances: League 500+1, FA Cup 45+1, League Cup 35, European 15, Others 12
Goals: League 6, FA Cup 1, League Cup 2, European 0, Others 1
Debut: League, 24 February 1968 v Newcastle United (a) lost 2–0

Also played for: Huddersfield Town, Stoke City, England (5 Under-23 caps)

Derek 'Squeak' Parkin was one of the best left-backs in the First Division for a decade – between 1969 and 1979 – and one feels if it hadn't been for Terry Cooper and future Wolves captain Emlyn Hughes he would surely have gained full international honours for England. He did represent his country in five Under-23 internationals and also played for the Football League, but a lot of people, including his fellow professionals, thought he deserved more honours than that.

A stylish defender, Parkin relied successfully on skill, interception and anticipation. He was lithe, not at all strong in physique, he tackled well and his distribution was first class. Hardly ever cautioned, his overall performances for Wolves were superb – and he had the honour and pleasure of becoming the first player ever to appear in 600 senior games for the club and also the first to top 500 in the Football League, reaching the latter milestone on 13 March 1982 at Villa Park.

A very consistent performer, Parkin appeared in 50 or more competitive games in a season for Wolves no fewer than five times (another record), was an ever present in League action on four occasions and had one run of 134 consecutive first-team outings from his debut (in his home town) until 14 November 1970.

Signed by manager Ronnie Allen on St Valentine's Day in 1968 for just £80,000 from Huddersfield Town, for whom he appeared in more than 60 League and Cup games, Parkin played at right-back with the Terriers. In fact, his first 15 games for Wolves were in the same position before new boss Bill McGarry (a former Huddersfield player incidentally) switched him to the left flank towards the end of the following season where he partnered Gerry Taylor and registered his first ever-present campaign. In 1969–70 he again played in every game (50), and, besides Taylor, both Bernard Shaw and Les Wilson occupied the right-back berth, Shaw becoming Derek's regular partner a year later when Wolves won the Texaco Cup.

In 1971–72 Wolves reached the Final of the UEFA Cup, but sadly for Parkin he missed out through injury, Shaw and Taylor manning the full-back positions in a 3–2 aggregate defeat.

As time progressed, Geoff Palmer came into the side to partner Parkin and, with the odd exception here and there due to injury, suspension and loss of form, they played extremely well together for some nine years, helping Wolves twice win the League Cup in 1974 and 1980, capture the Second Division Championship in 1977 (after suffering relegation the previous season), lose in the 1979 and 1981 FA Cup semi-finals to Arsenal and Spurs respectively, and he celebrated his 600th appearance for the club in a 1–0 home League win over Coventry City in November 1981.

Ian Greaves, who was coaching at Huddersfield when Parkin was there in the mid 1960s, took over the hot seat from John Barnwell in February 1982 to become the fifth manager he had played under at Molineux. And at that point he knew his time was up as a Wolves player, especially as John Humphrey and Palmer were holding down the two full-back positions with Mike Hollifield in reserve. After 14 years' service, he moved to Stoke City on a free transfer in March 1982, teaming up at the Victoria Ground with future Wolves player Alan Dodd and was soon to be joined by another ex-Molineux favourite George Berry. He went on to make 45 appearances for the Potters before retiring in May 1983 to concentrate on a new career in landscape gardening.

A splendid golfer, Parkin now resides in the same locality (near Shifnal) as former Wolves players Willie Carr and Bert Williams.

TEDDY PEERS

Date of birth: 31 December 1886, Connahs Quay, Flintshire
Died: 20 September 1935, Wolverhampton

Wolves record:
Appearances: League 186, FA Cup 12, Wartime 3
Goals: 0
Debut: League, 2 March 1912 v Glossop (h) drew 1–1

Also played for: Oswestry St Clare's, Chirk, Shrewsbury Town (trial), Connahs Quay Juniors, Connahs Quay Victoria, Connahs Quay, Stoke (World War One guest), Walsall (World War One guest), Hednesford Town (two spells), Port Vale, Wales (12 full caps, 1 Victory cap)

Goalkeeper Teddy Peers won several honours as a teenager – his three biggest coming in 1903 when he was the recipient of a Welsh Amateur Cup-winners' medal with Connahs Quay Juniors, in 1904 when he collected a Chester League Championship medal with Connahs Quays Victoria and in 1911 when he received a runners'-up prize after the town's premier club had been beaten 6–0 in the Welsh Cup Final by Wrexham. Despite conceding those half-dozen goals in that Final, he was immediately signed as an amateur by Wolves, who gave him his first outing in a junior match before the end of April, taking him on as a professional in July 1911.

Peers proved to be a loyal servant to the club, accumulating almost 200 first-team appearances. He took over from Frank Boxley towards the end of the 1911–12 season and was virtually an ever present over the next three years, having one excellent run of 71 consecutive first-team outings while helping Wolves finish 10th, ninth and fourth respectively in the Second Division up the outbreak of World War One. During the hostilities he played as a guest for both Walsall and Stoke, helping the Potteries club win the Lancashire Section Championship in 1917–18 when he appeared in 31 matches.

Like so many goalkeepers of his era, Peers – who always wore a rather tatty-looking flat cap – began as an outfield player, occupying the outside-right position and then switching to left-back before settling down between the posts at the age of 17.

Agile and consistent, he made full use of his enormous hands and was as safe as houses when dealing with high crosses, although at times he did choose to punch the ball rather than catch it, and when he did attempt the manoeuvre he got tremendous distance with his clearance, once sending the ball downfield and well beyond the halfway line.

Teddy, a jovial character, always cracking jokes, made 33 appearances in the first season after World War One but then, following a series of mediocre performances by his standards, when he seemed to lose his edge and concentration, he was replaced in the Wolves goal by Noel George immediately after a 1–0 win over Derby County in an FA Cup second round, second replay. He was bitterly disappointed, more so when he was sitting in the stand watching Wolves lose in that season's Cup Final to Tottenham Hotspur at Stamford Bridge.

Peers represented Wales in 12 full internationals, eight with Wolves – the first against Ireland in 1913. He won his last four with Port Vale, whom he joined in January 1922 (after six months with Hednesford Town) and was the first player from that club ever to win full international recognition. His last game for his country was against England 10 years after his first – but if the Vale management team had been more amenable to his release, he would, without doubt, have gained more caps at senior level. In between times he played in one Victory International for Wales against England in October 1919.

In January 1922 Peers left Molineux and joined Port Vale, for whom he made 58 League and FA Cup appearances, helping the Valiants win the Staffordshire Infirmary Cup before returning to Hednesford Town in May 1923, retiring three years later. After that, Teddy, who still attended Wolves home matches, kept a succession of public houses in Wolverhampton, the first being the New Inn on Bilston Road.

TED PHEASANT

Date of birth: 15 February 1877, Wednesbury
Died: 17 July 1910, Birmingham

Wolves record:
Appearances: League 159, FA Cup 9
Goals: League 19, FA Cup 0
Debut: League, 19 September 1896 v Derby County (a) lost 4–3

Also played for: Wednesbury Excelsior, Wednesbury Old Athletic, West Bromwich Albion

Ted 'Cock' Pheasant packed a great deal into his 33 years. Initially a bustling forward with two of his local teams, Wednesbury Excelsior and Wednesbury Old Athletic, he joined Wolves in August 1895 and turned professional within a matter of weeks after impressing in a series of pre-arranged trials and friendly matches. As he grew older, he expanded upwards and outwards, and inside two years he stood at 6ft 2in tall and tipped the scales at 15st. Yet he looked super-fit and was blessed with a terrific physique, seldom found in a player who could occupy two completely different positions, those of centre-half and centre-forward.

As hard as nails, Pheasant loved to be in the thick of the action, a formidable footballer who gave nothing less than 110 percent each and every time he entered the field of play. Quite often, with his short, greased-down hair, he would roll the sleeves of his jersey as high up his arms as possible and at times would let his socks slip down round his ankles, making him look as fearsome as possible to the opposing team.

After a breaking-in season at Molineux, when he appeared in several second-team matches, Pheasant starred in eight League games in 1896–97, scoring one goal, a crashing penalty in a 3–0 win at Sunderland. However, the following year he didn't get a look in owing to the form of centre-forward Billy Beats and inside-left Billy Smith. At this point Ted, who had already appeared as an emergency defender, was taken aside by manager Jack Addenbrooke who told him that he would be Wolves' next centre-half. He eventually took over from Billy Malpass and never looked back, and he went on to make almost 170 appearances for the club.

Pheasant played in 27 League and Cup games in 1898–99 and was an ever present in each of the next two campaigns, contributing a total of eight goals, six proving to be vital point-winning efforts with two of them being outright winners against Bury in December 1899 and Manchester City in January 1901, both at Molineux. Continuing to perform with aggression, determination and confidence, Ted – who was always called 'Cock' by his teammates and was paid a weekly wage of £3.10s (£3.50) – missed only one game in 1901–02 after injuring his knee at Stoke. He scored a hat-trick from the centre-half position in a 3–0 home win over Newcastle United – and it would be another 93 years before another Wolves player achieved the same feat! He received a specially designed gold medal for that treble, presented to him by club chairman Mr T.H. Slaney. He also turned down the chance of representing the Football League against the Irish League so that he could play in a League game for Wolves....such was his commitment to the club.

A twisted ankle and a niggling thigh strain sidelined Pheasant for two-thirds of the 1902–03 campaign, George Walker deputising most of the time. Unfortunately, these tedious injury worries continued to plague him and, after being given time off, he managed only 15 starts in 1903–04. As a result, and obviously concerned about his fitness, Wolves agreed to transfer him to neighbours West Bromwich Albion for £500 in November 1904. He replaced Jack Bowden at the heart of the Baggies defence, and although he was absent through injury several times, he made 152 senior appearances (22 goals scored) and played in the 1907 FA Cup semi-final defeat by Everton before moving to Leicester Fosse for £300 in July 1910.

Pheasant, who enjoyed beekeeping and gardening (he was a rose enthusiast) never played a single game for the Foxes. Two weeks after leaving The Hawthorns he was admitted to a Birmingham hospital with peritonitis, presumably contracted after diving into a canal to rescue someone from under a barge. Sadly he failed to recover from that illness and died at the age of 33. Hundreds turned out for his funeral in Darlaston.

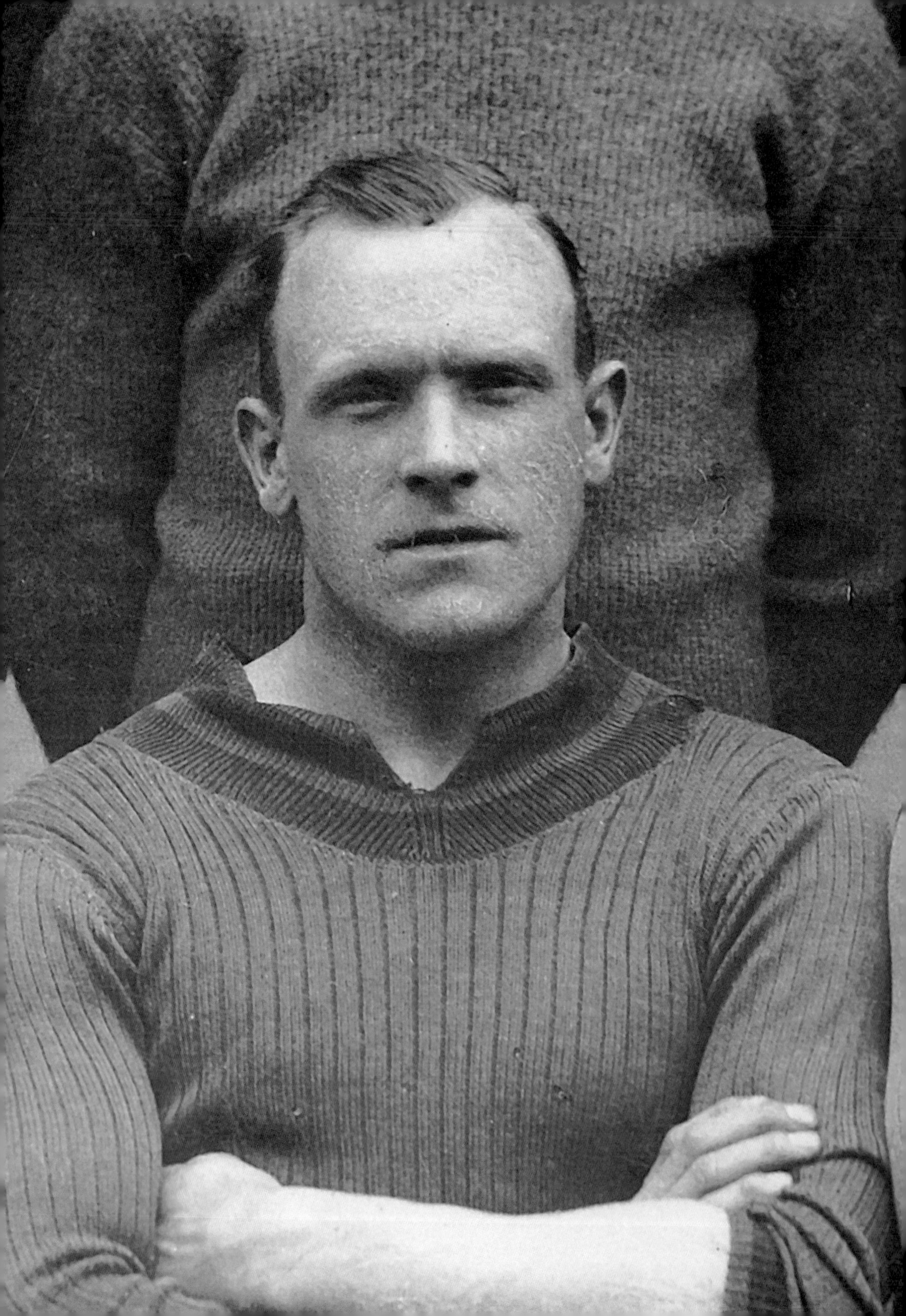

TOM PHILLIPSON

Date of birth: 31 October 1898, Ryton-on-Tyne, County Durham
Died: 19 November 1965, Wolverhampton

Wolves record:
Appearances: League 144, FA Cup 15
Goals: League 104, FA Cup 7
Debut: League, 25 December 1923 v Durham City (h) won 2–1

Also played for: Scotswood, Newcastle United, Swindon Town, Sheffield United, Bilston United, Walsall
Managed: Bilston United

After a wonderful career in junior football in the north east of England, Tom Phillipson became one of the greatest goalscorers in Wolves' history. In one junior match he netted 14 of his side's 15 goals and in his next outing got 10 out of 12. Capped twice by England as a schoolboy in 1913, he served in the West Yorkshire Regiment in Russia during World War One and in 1919 signed for his heroes Newcastle United. Yet surprisingly he never got going at St James' Park and after scoring four times in 15 outings joined Swindon Town for £500 in May 1921, switching to Molineux for £1,000 in December 1923.

Phillipson made his debut for Wolves 24 hours later, on Christmas Day against one of his former local clubs Durham City, and although he failed to score he set up a goal in a 2–1 victory as the Wanderers reinforced their position at the top of Division Three North. He only missed one game during the second half of that season, netting 14 goals, the first three coming in the shape of a hat-trick against another north-east team, Ashington, whom Wolves hammered 7–1. At the end of that campaign he celebrated with his colleagues as the Championship was won and with it Division Two status.

Absent from only six of the 44 competitive games in 1924–25, Phillipson was the team's top scorer with 16 goals but there was no promotion this time as Wolves finished sixth. In 1925–26 Tom, who by now had developed into a forceful centre-forward with great enthusiasm, commitment and a powerful right-foot shot, moved into overdrive and, despite missing 11 games before mid-December, he scored an amazing 37 goals. On Christmas Day Wolves visited Oldham Athletic, and up to that time he had netted just four times, but things changed dramatically at Boundary Park as he struck twice in a 2–1 win and incredibly failed to score in only five of the remaining 23 matches. He fired in hat-tricks against Middlesbrough and Stockport and cracked in four goals in a 7–1 thrashing of Barnsley. His efforts, though, were in vain as Wolves missed promotion again, finishing fourth, eight points behind runners-up Derby County.

There was disappointment yet again the following season as Wolves slumped to 15th in the table despite the scoring heroics of Phillipson. The club's leading marksman once more, his tally of 31 goals included another hat-trick against Barnsley, who were demolished 9–1 in November, a five-timer in a 7–2 home win over Bradford at Christmas and a treble in a 5–0 romp over Clapton Orient. In May 1927 Wolves parted company with manager Fred Scotchbrook, replacing him with Major Frank Buckley. The change of leadership seemed to affect Tom, and in 24 games that season he netted only 11 times, a fair rate but below what the Major expected from him.

Phillipson's final goal for the club (his 111th overall) came in a 2–1 home win over his favourite team Barnsley, and a week later, on 18 February 1928, he played his last game for Wolves as they lost 4–0 at West Bromwich Albion. Sheffield United had come in with a substantial offer for his services, one the Molineux board couldn't refuse and, much to the disappointment of the supporters, he moved to Bramall Lane for £2,600.

Never the same player again, Phillipson spent two seasons with the Blades, and after assisting Bilston United as player-manager and Walsall (1931–32) he retired to start his own business in Wolverhampton. He later entered local government and was appointed Mayor of the town in 1938. Very well-respected within the community, he died in 1965, aged 67.

JESSE PYE

Date of birth:	22 December 1919, Treeton, near Rotherham
Died:	19 February 1984, Blackpool

Wolves record:

Appearances:	League 188, FA Cup 20, Other 1
Goals:	League 90, FA Cup 5, Other 0
Debut:	League, August 1946 v Arsenal (h) won 6–1
Also played for:	Catliffe FC, Treeton FC, Sheffield United, Notts County, Luton Town, Derby County, Wisbech Town, England (1 full, 1 Victory cap)
Managed:	Wisbech Town

Able to play at inside right or centre-forward, Jesse Pye captivated Wolves supporters for six years with his delicate, subtle touches, mazy dribbling skills and incisiveness.

Admirably built for a front player, the dark haired, swarthy complexioned Yorkshireman had a brief pre-World War Two association with Sheffield United before joining Notts County in August 1945. He spent one excellent season with the Magpies, scoring 17 goals in 34 appearances in the transitional League and FA Cup competitions as well as playing for England in a Victory international against Belgium at Wembley, netting in a 2–0 win, before Wolves manager Ted Vizard paid a substantial amount of money (around £10,000) for his services in May 1946.

Pye proved to be an excellent capture, bagging a superb hat-trick on his debut in a gold shirt when Arsenal were thrashed 6–1 at Molineux on the opening day of the first official post-World War Two League campaign. He linked up in exciting fashion with Dennis Westcott and together they netted 60 goals in 1946–47, Westcott securing 39 to Jesse's 21, which included another treble in a 7–2 home drubbing of his future club Derby County.

The following season the lethal duo plus new recruit Sammy Smyth and an in-form Johnny Hancocks were magnificent, and between them rammed in another 46 goals, Pye contributing 16. Twelve months on and things got even better as Wolves went all the way to Wembley where they met Leicester City in the FA Cup Final, Pye grabbing two goals, one a classic header from Hancocks's magnificent cross, which some people believe was one of the greatest ever scored at the 'old' stadium.

Pye weighed in with a total of 21 goals in 1948–49 and added 19 more the following season when Wolves were pipped to the Championship by Portsmouth on goal average. In fact, Stan Cullis's men needed a cricket score at home to Birmingham City on their last match to sneak ahead of Pompey. They did pretty well and, with two more strikes from him, almost achieved the impossible with a 6–1 victory. He also gained his only full England cap this term, playing in that famous game at Goodison Park when the Republic of Ireland caused a major upset by winning 2–0.

In 1950–51 Pye suffered a spate of injuries and played in only 23 League games, scoring four times. He bounced back in style in 1951–52 and finished as top scorer with 15 goals in 30 games, playing alongside Roy Swinbourne and at times Dennis Wilshaw, aided and abetted by Jimmy Dunn and wingers Hancocks and Mullen. However, with so much forward talent available to the manager, he was allowed to leave Molineux, joining Luton Town in May 1952. He later assisted Derby County and Wisbech Town, eventually taking over as player-manager of the latter club. On quitting football in 1966, he became a hotelier in Blackpool. His League career realised 146 goals in 310 games.

DICKY RHODES

Date of birth: 18 February 1908, Wolverhampton
Died: 21 January 1993, Wolverhampton

Wolves record:
Appearances: League 149, FA Cup 7
Goals: League 10, FA Cup 0
Debut: League, 16 March 1929 v Chelsea (a) won 2–0

Also played for: Redditch United, Sheffield Wednesday, Swansea Town, Rochdale

Dickie Rhodes played for both Wolverhampton and England at Schoolboy level. At that time he was a centre-forward, scoring plenty of goals. He continued in the same vein after joining Redditch United in 1923 and in three seasons of non-League football netted 75 times.

Wolves had monitored his progress meticulously, and in July 1926 they offered Rhodes a professional contract at Molineux. He went on to serve Wolves for more than nine years, appearing on over 150 first-class games and gaining a Second Division Championship-winning medal in 1932.

Rhodes was converted into a right-half by Wolves' legendary manager Major Frank Buckley during the 1930–31 campaign, when George Lax was injured. He never looked back and held that position until Tom Smalley arrived on the scene in 1933, at which point Dicky slipped into the reserves but was always ready to step forward when required, whether to fill in for Smalley or, indeed, take over at left-half on the odd occasion. He was regarded as one of the best half-backs in the Second Division during the late 1920s to early 1930s, and one felt that if Wolves had been in the top flight at the time then Dicky may well have earned a full England cap.

A gifted footballer, possessing heart and energy, Rhodes was an exceptionally smart tackler, executing perfect timing, and above all he was thoughtful with his passing, very rarely using the long ball to find a colleague, preferring instead to play it short and precise. And he was also adept at keeping the ball in play when delivering a pass close to the touchline. He was very rarely spoken to by the referee – unusual in some respects for a defender!

Rhodes made his first League start as an emergency inside-right at Chelsea in March 1929 when Len Featherby and Francis Green were both out injured. The following season he made 11 senior appearances, all in the forward line, and scored five goals, the first coming on the same ground where, six months earlier, he had made his debut, Stamford Bridge. He also netted twice in a 4–0 home win over Cardiff City in the April.

In 1930–31 Rhodes played in 30 League and FA Cup games, establishing himself in the right-half berth and forming an excellent middle-line with Reg Hollingworth and Dai Richards. He was brilliant in home games against Bury, when he had a hand in three of the goals in a 7–0 win, and Nottingham Forest just after Christmas (won 4–2). He captained the side occasionally (in the absence of Wilf Lowton), and in 1931–32, when the Second Division title was won, he missed only two games. He appeared in roughly only half of Wolves' First Division fixtures the following season owing to a tedious knee injury, but he did have the pleasure of scoring in the top flight, helping his side beat Derby County 3–1 in the penultimate home League game.

With frequent changes being made to the team, Rhodes played in 45 competitive games over the next three seasons before the FA Cup holders Sheffield Wednesday beat off both Liverpool and Manchester City to secure his services for £3,200 in October 1935. Initially understudy to Wilf Sharp at Hillsborough, he was first choice in 1936–37 but lost his place to Fred Walker and moved to Swansea Town in exchange for Idris Lewis. The outbreak of World War Two effectively ended his career, and after the hostilities he returned to Wolverhampton to become 'mine host' of the Posada Inn. In his spare time he was a champion canary breeder – he won the national title in 1933 – as well as being a keen pigeon fancier.

JOHN RICHARDS

Date of birth: 9 November 1950, Warrington

Wolves record:
Appearances: League 365+20, FA Cup 42+2, League Cup 32+1, Europe 14, Others 8+2
Goals: League 144, FA Cup 24, League Cup 18, Europe 4, Others 4
Debut: League, 28 February 1970 v West Bromwich Albion (a) drew 3–3

Also played for: Derby County, Maritimo Funchal (Madiera), England (1 full, 2 Under-21 and 6 Under-23 caps)

Known as 'King John', 'JR' or 'Richie' by the Molineux fans, John Richards was a superb centre-forward, skilful, quick, alert and decisive. His total of 194 goals remained a club record until 1992 and earned him a place forever in the memories of those who saw him play.

Born in a Rugby League stronghold, Richards played both rugby and soccer at school but chose the round-ball game and represented Lancashire Grammar Schools, scoring six goals against an English Public Schools team in 1966. Scouts from various clubs started to take note of his goalscoring ability, and it was the Wolves man Tony Penman who informed chief scout Joe Gardiner about his prowess. After seeing off approaches from Derby County and Sheffield Wednesday, he was given a trial in a reserve game against Derby, and although he didn't score in a 4–0 win he was signed by Wolves the following week (July 1967), lodging in the same digs as youth coach Barry Powell.

Turning professional in July 1969, Richards's League debut followed seven months later in the Black Country derby at The Hawthorns, and he scored his first goal for the club in the Anglo-Italian Cup against Fiorentina at the end of that season. In September 1970 he claimed the first of his 144 League goals for Wolves as a substitute against Huddersfield at Molineux, and four months later he netted his first FA Cup goal in a match against Derby. The following season he made the number-nine shirt his own, scoring 16 times in 46 matches, 10 of which were in the UEFA Cup. Wolves reached the Final of that competition, only to lose on aggregate to Tottenham Hotspur. He scored against Academica Coimbra, Carl Zeiss Jena and Ferencvaros in previous rounds.

Now in excellent form, the 1972–73 season proved to be Richards's best in terms of goals scored, although it was to be one of great disappointment to him and his colleagues. Wolves finished fifth in the First Division but lost in the semi-finals of both the FA and League Cup competitions to Leeds United and Spurs respectively. His goal-tally was 37, of which 27 came in the League and included hat-tricks against Stoke and Everton. His efforts earned him his only full England cap in May of that season. Because of the political situation in Northern Ireland, the game was switched to Goodison Park, and there were plenty of Wolves fans in the 30,000 crowd to see John assist in both goals as England won 2–1. He also represented his country at Youth, Under-21 and Under-23 levels.

In 1973–74 Richards won his first medal with Wolves, who beat Manchester City 2–1 in the League Cup Final. He scored the winning goal with five minutes remaining – but it was the last of 18 he netted that season, because after that game he underwent a pelvic operation.

Wolves' leading marksman in six of the next seven seasons, during that time Richards also suffered the despair of relegation and the joy of immediate promotion as well as gaining a second League Cup-winners' medal when Wolves beat Nottingham Forest 1–0 in the 1980 Final. The elation of that victory was followed by two seasons of disappointment, Wolves being relegated again in 1982. At this juncture, his career at Molineux was nearing an end. He had a loan spell with Derby before making his final League appearance for Wolves in a 0–0 draw with Bolton at Molineux in April 1983.

Retiring after a spell in Madeira with the Portuguese Second Division side Maritimo Funchal, Richards took employment with the Wolverhampton Leisure Services Department before returning to Molineux as a director following the death of Billy Wright in 1994. Later appointed as the club's managing director, John held that position until the summer of 2000. He now works in sports ground development (West Midlands region).

WILLIAM CRISPIN ROSE

Date of birth: 3 April 1861, St Pancras, London
Died: 4 February 1937, Wolverhampton

Wolves record:
Appearances: League 134, FA Cup 21
Goals: 0
Debut: League, 19 January 1889 v Notts County (a) lost 3–0

Also played for: Small Heath, London Swifts, Preston North End, Stoke, Loughborough Town, England (5 caps)

Billy Crispin Rose was rightly regarded as one of the best goalkeepers of his time, and the fact that he was something of a psychologist, respecting opposing forwards, doubtlessly contributed to his brilliance. Larger than life and twice as eccentric, he was a big man, solid and strong. At times he was quite brilliant and always seemed to be in command of his area. He regularly chose to punch the ball clear rather than collect it safely in his hands, and on many occasions during the course of a game he would race out from his goal-mouth and fly-kick the ball upfield or into touch. He was brave and agile, had good positional sense, and although he never really suffered with injuries he did miss quite a few games for all of his clubs due to illness and international and representative call-ups.

Being from London, Rose was educated in the capital, but after leaving school he moved to the Midlands and joined Small Heath (now Birmingham City). However, he failed to make their first team, so he returned south to join the famous amateur side London Swifts early in 1883 and the following year won the first of five full caps for England, lining up against Ireland (won 8–1), Scotland (lost 1–0) and Wales (won 4–0). He continued to assist the Swifts up to February 1885 when he signed for Preston North End, switching to Stoke shortly afterwards and then on to Wolves in January 1889.

Taking over from John Baynton, Rose played in the last four games of that inaugural League season (1888–89) and was absent only once in the next three campaigns, helping Wolves twice finish fourth in the table and then claim sixth spot in 1891–92. Challenged for the number-one slot by Joshua Hassall during the first half of 1892–93, he missed a few games through injury but when fit was quickly back in the firing line, his name seemingly being one of the first on the team sheet. He maintained a high level of consistency throughout his career and was in superb form during Wolves' FA Cup run of 1893 when they went all the way to the Final and met Everton at Fallowfield, Manchester. Prior to that game, which took place in front of a then-record crowd for a final, 45,000, he had conceded only four goals in five previous rounds, and he said publicly that he would keep a clean sheet in the Final. He did precisely that as Wolves beat the Merseysiders 1–0, Harry Allen scoring the goal.

Still in control at the start of the next campaign, Rose – who was instrumental in forming the Players' Union (now the PFA) – was eventually replaced by Hassall in February 1894 after conceding 12 goals in four games. He joined Loughborough Town soon afterwards but returned to Wolves for a second spell in the summer of 1895, playing in 21 competitive games before losing out to new signing Billy Tennant. At the end of the season he retired and later became a publican in Birmingham and then in Wolverhampton, as well as running a corner shop in Bordesley, near St Andrew's. He was 75 years of age when he died.

ALEC SCOTT

Date of birth: 29 October 1913, Liverpool
Died: 1962, Wolverhampton

Wolves record:
Appearances: League 110, FA Cup 10, Wartime 85
Goals: 0
Debut: League, 8 February 1936 v Derby County (h) drew 0–0

Also played for: Forest Dynamos, Liverpool, Burnley, Aston Villa (guest), Southport (guest), Crewe Alexandra

Goalkeeper Alec Scott cost Wolves £1,250 when signed from Burnley in February 1936. He was only 22 years of age at the time but had already appeared in 65 competitive games for the Clarets, having been a reserve at Liverpool prior to that.

Tall, well built and eminently safe with a huge kick, he brought a secure style of goalkeeping to Molineux which was to be of inestimable value over the next 10 years, during which time he made 129 senior appearances for Wolves as well as taking part in another 85 regional League and Cup games during World War Two when he also played as a guest for Aston Villa and Southport and represented an All British XI in 1939–40, having earlier played for a Football League XI.

The recipient of two First Division runners'-up medals with Wolves in successive seasons, 1937–38 and 1938–39, Scott also collected an FA Cup-runners'-up medal at the end of that latter campaign when, despite producing some fine saves, he couldn't prevent Portsmouth from beating the favourites Wolves 4–1 in the Final and causing a major upset.

Originally a centre-half, Scott represented England Boys in that position as a 14-year-old and besides enjoying his football with Forest Dynamoes he was also a fine pitcher at baseball, turning out regularly for his local team Oakmere in Liverpool's very competitive Zingari League.

Standing at 6ft 4in tall and weighing over 14st, Scott joined the groundstaff at Anfield in the summer of 1930, and by coincidence there was already another goalkeeper by the same name registered with the Reds – one Elisha Scott, the great Irish international who became a great friend of his. The South African Arthur Riley was also at the club, acting as first reserve, and, therefore, he found it hard going to break into the first team. Seeking first-team action, he eventually moved to Turf Moor in May 1933, and after helping Burnley reach the FA Cup semi-final two years later he switched his allegiance to Molineux where he replaced Jack Weare.

In the space of a fortnight in December 1936, Scott had the misfortune to get sent off twice when playing against different Yorkshire clubs – Leeds United (away) and Huddersfield Town (home). Although the first game was subsequently abandoned while he was still in the bath, with Wolves ahead 1–0, his manager Major Frank Buckley wasn't at all pleased when he was dismissed against Huddersfield because the 10 men of Wolves eventually lost the game 4–0. After that second indiscretion he was fined a week's wages (£8) on top of his eight-day suspension imposed by the League. He was handed a five-day ban for his initial misdemeanour against Leeds, which also earned him a £2 fine. Bob was back between the posts for the 'replay' against the latter club later in the season, which Wolves won 1–0.

After World War Two Bert Williams became Wolves' first-choice 'keeper, at which point Scott moved to pastures new, joining Crewe Alexandra in August 1947. He made almost 50 senior appearances for the Railwaymen before announcing his retirement from League football in June 1949. He later ran a general store on Dunstall Road, Whitmore Reans, Wolverhampton, and later served as a constable and then a detective in the local police force.

HAROLD SHAW

Date of birth: 22 May 1905, Hednesford, Staffs.
Died: 7 June 1984, Cannock, Staffs

Wolves record:
Appearances: League 235, FA Cup 14
Goals: 0
Debut: League, 25 August 1923 v Chesterfield (a) drew 0–0

Also played for: Hednesford Town, Sunderland

What a great full-back Harold Shaw was. Equally capable on either flank, he was a no-nonsense tackler, an inspirational leader, as fair and reliable as the day's long and described as 'a stylist of the first water'. He served Wolves exceedingly well for seven years before joining Sunderland, playing in one game when the Wearsiders won the League Championship in his last season before his enforced retirement through injury in May 1936. He remained at Roker Park as a coach for another two years.

Shaw was only 15 and working as an engineer's fitter when he won a place in Hednesford Town's first team. He went on to produce some very competent performances in a tough local League, and after Wolves had monitored his progress over a period of four months he joined the Molineux professional ranks in May 1923, signed by manager George Jobey.

Having just been relegated, Jobey was looking to change things round, and besides Shaw he also recruited other players including outside-left Evan Edwards from Merthyr Town, who was to become a great friend of Harold's. Both players went straight into the team at left-back and outside-left respectively, replacing George Marshall and Len Rhodes for Wolves' first-ever game in the Third Division North.

The baby of the side, Shaw was outstanding as partner to Ted Watson. He missed only five League games as Wolves won the Third Division North Championship at the first attempt, winning 24 matches and conceding only 27 goals.

Playing at a higher level the following season, Shaw continued to impress. He made 31 appearances in the League side as Wolves finished a very creditable sixth in the table, but well off the pace in terms of challenging for promotion. By now he was regarded as a class defender. He was confident and consistent and played even better in 1925–26 as Wolves edged up to fourth place in the Second Division, again falling just short of those clubs chasing promotion.

Watson was proving to be a great companion as Shaw steadily piled up his tally of games. He reached the personal milestone of 100 League appearances for Wolves at home to Clapton Orient in April 1926 and followed that up with his 150th at Oldham in November 1927 and his 200th came at Notts County in April 1929, the former Sheffield Wednesday and Stockport County defender Len Williams having taken over from Watson at right-back during the latter campaign.

After starring in 30 League and Cup games the following season, Shaw was surprisingly transferred by Major Frank Buckley to Sunderland for a substantial fee of £7,000 in February 1930 and was immediately thrown into the cauldron of a Tyneside-Wearside derby at St James' Park just 24 hours after his move. He later played in a fourth-round FA Cup replay against Derby County in March 1933, which attracted a record crowd of 75,118 to Roker Park. He remained a regular in the Sunderland team until a knee injury forced him to retire at the age of 31, having appeared in 217 senior games for Sunderland (two goals scored, both penalties).

Often considered unlucky not to gain representative honours, the nearest Shaw came to a full cap was to play for England against The Rest in an international trial before he left Molineux.

In later years he returned to the Midlands and became a member of the South Staffs and Penn golf club while also working at Cannock colliery. He was 79 when he died.

BILL SHORTHOUSE

Date of birth: 27 May 1922, Bilston

Wolves record:
Appearances: League 344, FA Cup 30, Others 2, Wartime 3
Goal: League 1, FA Cup 0, Others 0, Wartime 0
Debut: League South, 20 December 1941, Walsall (a) won 2–1

Also played for: St Martin's Old Boys

Bill Shorthouse had the unenviable task of taking over from Stan Cullis at centre-half in the Wolves defence. He took to it like a duck to water and went on to give the club supreme service. Teammate Roy Swinbourne said 'Bill was strong but always fair' and another colleague, Dennis Wilshaw, thought he was 'One helluva of good player.'

Signed as an amateur by Wolves from St Martin's Old Boys, Shorthouse made his first appearance for the club at left-half in a regional wartime game against Walsall in December 1941 before enlisting as a soldier with the Royal Engineers. In June 1944 he took part in the D-Day landings in Normandy with the initial ground troops, but four hours later was taken off the beaches, badly wounded, and transported to a nearby French hospital. He returned to England, recovered from his injuries, and after playing for Wolves' Central League side and for Wath Wanderers (the club's nursery team) he made his First Division debut at left-back at the start of the 1947–48 campaign, a position he filled with great efficiency at the outset of his career and also at the end after his excellent spell at centre-half.

Within two months of making his debut, Shorthouse was switched to the heart of the Wolves defence and, in fact, gave away a penalty in his first game in the number-five jersey against Arsenal, Ronnie Rooke converting from the spot to earn the Gunners a point from a 1–1 draw.

A wholehearted and thoroughly genuine footballer, big and stocky, Shorthouse, who was nicknamed 'The Baron' and 'Shorty' by his teammates, possessed tremendous grit and resilience. He was strong and positive with his challenges, never shirked a tackle, was consistent and reliable and missed only 32 League games out of a possible 378 between October 1947 and September 1956, making 40 appearances in Wolves' Championship-winning season of 1953–54 when he was outstanding in a very professional Wolves side. He was only ever out of the side through injury; he was never dropped and received very few cautions. When he switched back to full-back in 1955 his place at centre-half went to England player Billy Wright. He scored only one goal for Wolves – a blockbusting drive to clinch a 2–0 League victory over Charlton Athletic at Molineux in November 1955 – but did hit the bar in a local derby against West Bromwich Albion and came near to finding the net (from a corner) in an FA Cup tie against Liverpool in February 1949, former Wolves 'keeper Cyril Sidlow saving his goal-bound effort.

In October 1951, Shorthouse came close to winning a full England cap, but in the end Malcolm Barrass of Bolton got the nod for the game against Wales in Cardiff. He was never considered again, although he was named as a reserve for the Football League XI.

After retiring in May 1957, after 16 years as a player, Shorthouse was appointed coach at Molineux. He later took similar positions with neighbours Birmingham City and Aston Villa, guiding the youngsters of the latter club to victory in the 1980 FA Youth Cup Final. He also worked in the same capacity with the England youth team in 1970–71. He is still living in the West Midlands, having recently moved from Penn where he resided for several years.

BILL SLATER, OBE, CBE, BSc

Date of birth: 29 April 1927, Clitheroe, Lancashire

Wolves record:
Appearances: League 310, FA Cup 23, Europe 1
Goals: League 24, FA Cup 6, Europe 0
Debut: League, 4 October 1952 v Manchester United (h) won 6–2

Also played for: Yorkshire Amateurs, Blackpool, Brentford, Northern Nomads, England (12 full, 8 amateur caps)

Bill Slater was an amateur when he played inside-left for Blackpool in the 1951 FA Cup Final against Newcastle United. He finished on the losing side that day, but nine years later he gained a winners' medal in the same competition when he skippered Wolves to a 3–0 victory over Blackburn Rovers from the centre-half position, having been converted into a steady, reliable defender by manager Stan Cullis.

As a schoolboy Slater shared the same enthusiasm as his friends but never gained any fame or reward for his efforts. In fact, he never dreamed of playing the game for money. However, on leaving school he signed amateur forms for Blackpool while also taking employment as a bank clerk in his home town. Called up for National Service, his interest in the game was incubated still further, and when he was demobbed he joined Yorkshire Amateurs. Yes, a Yorkshire team, although he was a Lancastrian, for he was, by now, studying to become a physical training instructor at Leeds University.

Still in contract with Blackpool, Slater's ties became rather stretched when he graduated and accepted a post at Birmingham University. The trip to Blackpool was a rather long journey, especially as he was still an amateur, receiving only expenses and also his fiancee was living in London. He was torn between the two stools, and after scoring 12 goals in 35 appearances for the Seasiders he decided to join his fiancee in London and joined Brentford in December 1951. His stay at Griffin Park was only brief, and in August 1952 he moved back to the Midlands to join Wolves. He became a semi-professional in February 1954.

After a fine debut against the reigning champions Manchester United in front of almost 40,000 fans at Molineux, a game Wolves won handsomely 6–2, Slater made steady but worthwhile progress in the First Division and gained a League Championship-winning medal in 1953–54, missing only three matches while occupying the right-half position with England's Billy Wright alongside him. Over the next six years Bill, tall and confident, played exceedingly well, but so did Wolves – and although there was an abundance of half-back talent at Molineux, the ever-reliable Slater was always included in the side – when fit of course! He also became a valuable member of the England squad and in the 1958 World Cup Finals in Sweden was part of an all-Wolves half-back line in games against USSR, Brazil and Austria. The two other Wolves players were skipper Wright and Eddie Clamp.

Two more Championship-winning medals came Slater's way, in 1958 and 1959, followed, of course, by victory in the Cup Final, after which he gained a BSc degree at University and was voted Footballer of the Year, although he had started that Cup-winning season out of the first team.

In the summer of 1963, with Wolves well off for half-backs with the likes of Johnny Kirkham, Dave Woodfield, Ron Flowers, George Showell and Fred Goodwin, Slater returned to Griffin Park, having served Wolves for 11 years. After a season with the Bees he played for Northern Nomads before retiring in the summer of 1965, aged 38. Soon afterwards Bill became deputy director of the Crystal Palace Sports Centre (London) and later worked as director of PE at both Liverpool and Birmingham Universities. In 1982 he was awarded the OBE for services to sport and in 1998 received the CBE.

For five years from 1984, Slater, who now lives in London, was director of National Services and in July 1989 was elected president of the British Gymnastics Association. Engaged thereafter as a member of the National Olympic Committee, he also sat on the panel of the National Lottery. His daughter Barbara was a former national champion gymnast and represented Britain in the 1976 Olympic Games and later worked for Central TV.

An interesting chapter in Bill's footballing career came on 2 May 1956. At the time he was studying to become a PTI at Birmingham University and an aeroplane was chartered to fly him north for an evening League game away at Sheffield United. His manager, Cullis, wanted him there, no questions asked. The Auster pilot was unable to locate the landing strip and when the aircraft finally came down, unheralded at the RAF aerodrome at Worksop, it was immediately surrounded by fire-tenders, ambulances and angry security officers. When Wolves kicked-off against the Blades, Bill was still hitch-hiking a lift to Bramall Lane, having been replaced in the team by George Showell! A not-too-happy manager saw his side draw 3–3 with the Blades and as a result finished third in the table, whereas a win would have seen them finish runners-up to Manchester United.

GOOD YEA

MIKE STOWELL

Date of birth: 19 April 1965, Preston, Lancashire

Wolves record:
Appearances: League 384+1, FA Cup 30, League Cup 22, Others 11
Goals: 0
Debut: League, 18 March 1989 v Bury (h) won 4–0

Also played for: Leyland Motors, Preston North End, Chester City, York City, Manchester City, Port Vale, Bristol City

Mike Stowell holds the record for making the most appearances in senior football for Wolves as a goalkeeper, accumulating a total of 448 – 28 more than former England international Bert Williams. He joined Preston North End as a professional from non-League side Leyland Motors in February 1985 but was unable to get into the first team at Deepdale, and after 10 months without a game he moved to Goodison Park on a free transfer, signed by manager Howard Kendall as cover for Welsh international Neville Southall.

With Southall in command of the number-one position, Stowell was farmed out on loan by Everton to gain experience, and over a period of five years (1985–90) he assisted, in turn, Chester City, York City, Manchester City, Port Vale, Wolves and his former club Preston. Surprisingly, in that period of time he made only 55 first-class appearances, including seven for the Third Division champions elect Wolves. The first of these was against Bury in March 1989 when he deputised for the injured Mark Kendall in a 4–0 win, Steve Bull scoring a hat-trick. He played very well in his second match against his former club Chester (1–1), and he also saved his side from defeat in another drawn game at Cardiff.

It would be another 15 months, however, before Stowell moved to Molineux on a permanent basis, eventually being signed for £250,000 by manager Graham Turner in June 1990 to replace Kendall. He made his 'second' debut for the club at the start of that season, in a 3–2 home defeat by Oldham Athletic. He stood at 6ft 2in tall and weighed over 14st at his peak, and he was a fine shot-stopper with splendid reflexes and good positional sense. In November 1990 he went out and hired a tractor to beat the severe snow storms in the Midlands in order to link up with the England B team ahead of a friendly international with Algeria, which never materialised due to the atrocious weather. He loved his football and this proved it. He missed only seven League games that season and was an ever present in 1991–92 (51 games) before suffering injury worries and loss of form in 1992–93 when both Dave Beasant and Paul Jones deputised. However, he was back at his best the following season, appearing in all of Wolves' 55 competitive matches, conceding just over a goal a game (58), and he was in fine form again in 1994–95 when Wolves were beaten by Bolton Wanderers in the First Division Play-off semi-final.

The 1995–96 season proved to be a much tougher campaign for Stowell, and indeed for Wolves. In fact, he was quite brilliant in several games, including those against West Bromwich Albion (home and away), Luton Town at Kenilworth Road, Millwall at The Den and Oldham Athletic at Boundary Park, and in the end he gained a lot of credit from his manager and colleagues alike as demotion to the Second Division was avoided by just three points.

Mark McGhee moved in as manager halfway through that season, and in 1996–97 he was delighted with the form shown by Stowell, who was once again an ever present between the posts as Wolves disappointingly lost in the Play-offs again, this time to Crystal Palace, having finished three places above the London side in the final League table.

Over the next two seasons Stowell missed only a handful of matches before Michael Oakes, formerly of Aston Villa, took over the goalkeeping duties, sending him into the reserves. He finally left Molineux in June 2001, signed on a free transfer by Bristol City. He remained at Ashton Gate for four years and was 40 years of age when he announced his retirement in June 2005, having amassed a career total of 525 club appearances.

EDDIE STUART

Date of birth:	12 May 1931, Johannesburg, South Africa

Wolves record:

Appearances:	League 287, FA Cup 21, Europe 11, Others 3
Goals:	League 1, FA Cup 0, Others 0
Debut:	League, 15 April 1952 v West Bromwich Albion (h) lost 4–1
Also played for:	Johannesburg Rangers, Stoke City, Tranmere Rovers, Stockport County, Worcester City
Managed:	Worcester City

Eddie Stuart began playing football at the age of eight. His progress was rapid, doing very well at schoolboy level and also with Johannesburg Rangers, with whom he won the South African Cup. When he was 18 his coach at Rangers, Billy Butler, a former player with Bolton Wanderers, along with his father, persuaded him to join Wolves (instead of Aston Villa), Stan Cullis signing him as a professional in January 1951.

Stuart's first game in a Wolves shirt was at centre-half in a reserve-team fixture away to West Bromwich Albion on the last day of the 1950–51 season, and he continued playing at the heart of the second strings' defence right up until he made his senior debut, ironically also against the Baggies, in April 1952 when he deputised for Roy Swinbourne at centre-forward, scoring his only goal for the club in a 4–1 defeat. At the end of the season he went home to celebrate his 21st birthday with his family and friends, but unfortunately, on the return journey, he picked up a tropical virus which doctors couldn't diagnose. He was admitted to Wolverhampton's Queen Victoria Nursing Institute, but his health didn't improve, so the club arranged for his mother to be flown out to be at his bedside. Slowly but surely, the strong-willed and determined player (who at one stage was given just two hours to live) regained full fitness, and after a year out of the game he returned to reserve-team action at the end of the 1952–53 campaign and went on to serve Wolves for another nine years, amassing well over 300 appearances.

Occupying predominantly the right-back position, Stuart made some outstanding performances, figuring in the last 12 games of Wolves' Championship-winning season of 1953–54. Unfortunately, for all his efforts, he didn't gain a medal. Earlier that season he had the pleasure of captaining Wolves in the first floodlit game at Molineux against the tourists from his native South Africa. Over the next three seasons he missed only 26 competitive games, helping Wolves finish second, third and sixth respectively in Division One. But in 1957–58 he finally got his hands on his first prize, a League Championship medal, after some quality performances alongside Gerry Harris at full-back.

The following season Stuart collected his second League-winners' medal and, like the rest of his colleagues, also made his European debut against the West German side FC Schalke 04. Unfortunately Wolves lost the two-leg tie 4–3 on aggregate.

The last season of the decade ended in disappointment for Stuart. After helping Wolves win the Charity Shield at the start of the campaign, he held his position in the side right up until the turn of the year but was replaced by George Showell. He returned for the odd game here and there but was denied the chance of playing in the 3–0 FA Cup Final win over Blackburn Rovers. 'As twelfth man, I received a winners' medal, but it wasn't the same' he said.

Undeterred, Stuart came back strongly, and over the next two seasons played in 74 out of 93 first-team games before moving to pastures new, joining Stoke City in July 1962 for £8,000. Named as skipper by manager Tony Waddington, his experience and leadership helped the Potters win the Second Division title in his first season at the club. In August 1964 he switched to Tranmere Rovers for £4,000 and spent two seasons at Prenton Park before ending his League career with Stockport County, gaining a Fourth Division Championship medal in 1967. After an excellent spell as player-manager at Worcester City, for whom he starred in over 100 games, he retired in 1970 with 565 senior appearances under his belt. He became a successful businessman and lived in his adopted Wolverhampton until 2006 when he moved to North Wales.

ROY SWINBOURNE

Date of birth: 25 August 1929, Denaby Main, Yorkshire

Wolves record:
Appearances: League 211, FA Cup 18, Charity Shield 1
Goals: League 107, FA Cup 2, Charity Shield 2
Debut: League, 17 December 1949 v Fulham (h) drew 1–1

Also played for: Huddersfield Town (amateur), Wath Wanderers

Roy Swinbourne's career in professional football was all too short. Tragically, he was forced to retire through injury in the summer of 1957, three months before his 28th birthday.

Once an amateur with Huddersfield Town, Swinbourne joined Wolves at the age of 15 and played for the club's nursery side Wath Wanderers before turning professional on his 17th birthday in 1946. Developing quickly, he had established himself in the second XI by 1947 and made his League debut against Fulham in December 1949 when he deputised for Dennis Wilshaw, Jesse Pye switching to the inside-left position. Retaining his place, he scored his first goal for the club in his third game (against Aston Villa) and ended the season with eight to his name, including his first in the FA Cup in a 3–0 home win over Plymouth Argyle. He was top scorer in 1950–51 with 22 goals in the League and Cup, claiming his first senior hat-trick in a 7–1 home win over Bolton Wanderers.

Quick, alert, with a terrific first touch, Swinbourne was also exceptionally strong in the air and thrived on teasing crosses from both wings, and Hancocks and Mullen provided plenty of these. He struggled at times with injuries in 1951–52, but he was back to his best the following season when he netted 21 goals as Wolves finished third in Division One. By now Swinbourne, Dennis Wilshaw and Peter Broadbent were the main three centre-forward players, and there is no doubt that Wolves were one of the strongest teams in the country, certainly in attack. This was clearly emphasised in 1953–54 when, for the first time in the club's history, the coveted League Championship Trophy found its way to Molineux, Roy contributing greatly to that triumph with 24 goals, a haul that included five twos and a three. The next season he represented England B against West Germany in March 1955, playing with Duncan Edwards and Johnny Haynes. He also netted another 18 goals as Wolves just failed to retain their crown and then, after just 13 games at the start of the next season, injury struck, initially at Kenilworth Road followed by a second at Deepdale. He suffered badly-torn knee ligaments during Wolves' First Division League game at Luton in November 1955, falling awkwardly as he tried to avoid a photographer at the side of the goal. After some intense treatment he returned to action for the match at Preston four weeks later, but unfortunately two minutes from the end of that fixture his knee gave way, and he never played again, eventually becoming a local referee and working for the Goodyear Tyre Company.

Prior to those mishaps, Swinbourne had been in magnificent form. He had already bagged 17 goals, smashing four past Manchester City and netting hat-tricks against Cardiff City at Ninian Park (when Wolves won 9–1 to equal the First Division record set in 1909 by Sunderland against Newcastle United in 1908) and Huddersfield Town, and these three feats were all achieved on successive Saturdays.

Chatting with Roy a few years ago at a reunion of former Wolves players, he recalled 'It was a body blow when I was told that I must retire. If I don't I could be a cripple before I reach the age of 40. I had to abide by the doctor's orders. I had seen a bit of the world, visited South Africa and played with and against some of the greatest footballers of that time. It was great fun while it lasted.'

Swinbourne now lives in retirement in the village of Kinver near Stourbridge.

NUTMEG
GOODYEAR

ANDY THOMPSON

Date of birth:	9 November 1967, Featherstone, Staffordshire
Wolves record:	
Appearances:	League 356+20, FA Cup 20, League Cup 22, Others 33
Goals:	League 43, FA Cup 1, League Cup 0, Others 1
Debut:	League, 22 November 1986 v Wrexham (h) lost 3–0
Also played for:	West Bromwich Albion, Tranmere Rovers, Crewe Alexandra, Cardiff City, Shrewsbury Town, Hednesford Town

For such a small man, Andy Thompson proved to be a very capable full-back, tough and solid, quick and decisive, who loved to overlap down the left flank. A fine crosser of the ball (given the chance), he packed a powerful shot and was an expert penalty-taker – although he did miss some vital ones in a lengthy career.

Given his debut in midfield by West Bromwich Albion manager Nobby Stiles in the Full Members' Cup tie against Chelsea in November 1985 (when he scored in the penalty shoot-out), Thompson was never able to establish himself in the first XI and a year later, after 26 outings, was transferred to Wolves with striker Steve Bull in a deal worth £70,000, Andy being valued at £20,000.

Just prior to his arrival at Molineux, Wolves, who were lying in 11th position in Division Four, had been held to a 1–1 draw at home by non-League Chorley in an FA Cup first-round replay. Manager Graham Turner was a happy man when Thompson arrived. His midfield was not functioning and the fans weren't at all happy – indeed, less than 4,000 had attended the previous home League game with Rochdale and only 4,790 saw the Chorley replay. These were certainly tough times at Molineux and things had to improve or else!

Thompson and Bull made their first appearances for Wolves together in the home game against Wrexham on 22 November 1986. It wasn't a happy occasion. Wolves lost 3–0 and 48 hours later they were humiliated by Chorley in the second replay at Bolton, losing by the same score. And straightaway they suffered another 3–0 defeat at Lincoln. Things were going from bad to worse. Thankfully for all concerned, 'Bully' started to score goals, Thompson got to grips with things in midfield, and, from a position of anxiety, Wolves shot up the table and finished fourth but missed out on promotion after losing to Aldershot in the two-leg Play-off Final.

At this juncture, Thompson was still occupying a midfield role, but the left-back position was causing some concern. Five different players were used there in 1986–87, including Andy, and it was no surprise when Turner handed him the number-three shirt on a permanent basis six games into the next campaign. He never looked back and was outstanding that season as Wolves won the Fourth Division title and also the Sherpa Van Trophy at Wembley. An ever present in 1988–89 as Wolves took the Third Division title by eight points from Sheffield United, he played his part in 1989–90 as Wolves bedded themselves into a mid-table position in Division Two. He also reached the personal milestone of 150 League appearances for the club. Consistency was proving to be his greatest asset – and he avoided serious injury, missing the odd game here and there with knee and ankle problems, while also sitting out a few others when suspension kicked in. When in the team, he proved to be a great competitor, appearing in 49 out of 51 games in 1990–91.

Unfortunately Thompson had his worst season as a professional in 1991–92, injuries seriously affecting his performances. He played in only 19 matches as Wolves claimed 11th place in Division Two, 10 points off the Play-offs. Unable to hold his place in 1992–93, when again Wolves finished in mid-table, he was at his best again the following year, but sadly for him and his colleagues Wolves missed out on the Play-offs by three points after winning only one of their last four League games.

In 1994–95 Wolves did reach the Play-offs, but, with the Premiership beckoning, they were knocked out by Bolton Wanderers in the semi-final. Amazingly, 12 months later Wolves found themselves battling to stay up. But Thompson's experience helped them survive as he passed the milestone of 400 first-team appearances for the club.

Andy – who was granted a testimonial match versus Chelsea in 1996 – spent one more season at Molineux before moving to Tranmere Rovers, later assisting Crewe Alexandra (loan), Cardiff City, whom he helped gain promotion to the Second Division, Shrewsbury Town (loan) and Hednesford Town. He retired in 2005.

BOBBY THOMSON

Date of birth: 5 December 1943, Smethwick, Staffordshire

Wolves record:
Appearances: League 277+1, FA Cup 20, League Cup 2
Goals: League 2, FA Cup 1, League Cup 0
Debut: FA Cup, 27 January 1962 v West Bromwich Albion (h) lost 2–1

Also played for: Birmingham City, Walsall, Luton Town, Connecticut Bicentennials and Memphis Rogues (NASL), Worcester City, Stafford Rangers, Brewood, Solihull Borough, Tipton Town, England (8 caps)

Full-back Bobby Thomson was plucked from schoolboy football by Wolves' manager Stan Cullis at the start of the 1960s – and the clean-cut boy from Smethwick, who was a West Bromwich Albion supporter – did not take long to make his mark at Molineux. He moved up to the professional ranks in July 1961 and halfway through that season was called up for his first-team debut, in a fourth-round FA Cup tie against Wolves' Black Country neighbours Albion, taking over from Phil Kelly. Despite having a pretty quick winger up against him in Alec Jackson, he played well, although it wasn't a happy day for Thomson as the Baggies won 2–1 in front of 46,411 spectators at Molineux.

However, playing now in a team that was gradually declining from the halcyon days of the 1950s, Thomson gave the loyal supporters something to cheer about even though all around him things were not exactly happy! His big asset was his astonishing burst of speed, which not only allowed him scope for some modicum of attack but also to recover and amaze opponents by being back in defence to cover even when ostensibly beaten.

Thomson, making excellent progress, developed into one of the game's outstanding attacking full-backs, and he was duly rewarded with eight full England caps in the space of 13 months between November 1963 and December 1964. He made his international debut at left-back, in place of future World Cup winner Ray Wilson, against Northern Ireland at Wembley (won 8–3) and then starred in a 10–0 victory over the USA in New York before starring against Portugal, Argentina, Northern Ireland (again), Belgium, Wales and Holland. Unfortunately, when Alf Ramsey took over as England manager he was left out in the cold, the former Ipswich Town boss choosing to go with George Cohen and Wilson as his regular full-backs.

Even so, the name Bobby Thomson was always one of the first to be pencilled on the Wolves team sheet, right up to March 1969 when he moved across the Midlands to Birmingham City, signed by his former boss Stan Cullis, who had been such a major influence in his footballing career and, indeed, his life.

Thomson's last days at Molineux had not been as rosy as the first. Wolves had been relegated from the top flight but bounced back within two years and now there were many changes taking place inside the club. He had lost his way under manager Ronnie Allen and, in fact, his once permanent place had become less secure.

At first things went well at St Andrew's, but after Cullis's departure, early in 1970, football again started to leave a nasty taste in Thomson's mouth. It culminated in a near three-month loan to Walsall over the turn of the year in 1971, and following his return to Birmingham he was subsequently transferred to Luton Town, as Hatters boss Harry Haslam started to assemble a promotion-winning side at Kenilworth Road.

Thomson spent four years with Luton, for whom he made over 120 senior appearances. He also had a loan spell in the North America Soccer League with Connecticut Bicentennials (formerly Hartford) before ending his Football League career with Port Vale. Afterwards he assisted Worcester City, Stafford Rangers (as player-manager), Memphis Rogues (NASL), Brewood, Solihull Borough and Tipton Town and also appeared in several charity matches, mostly for the WBA All Stars. He ran a sportswear shop in Sedgley near Wolverhampton for many years and is now living in the West Midlands.

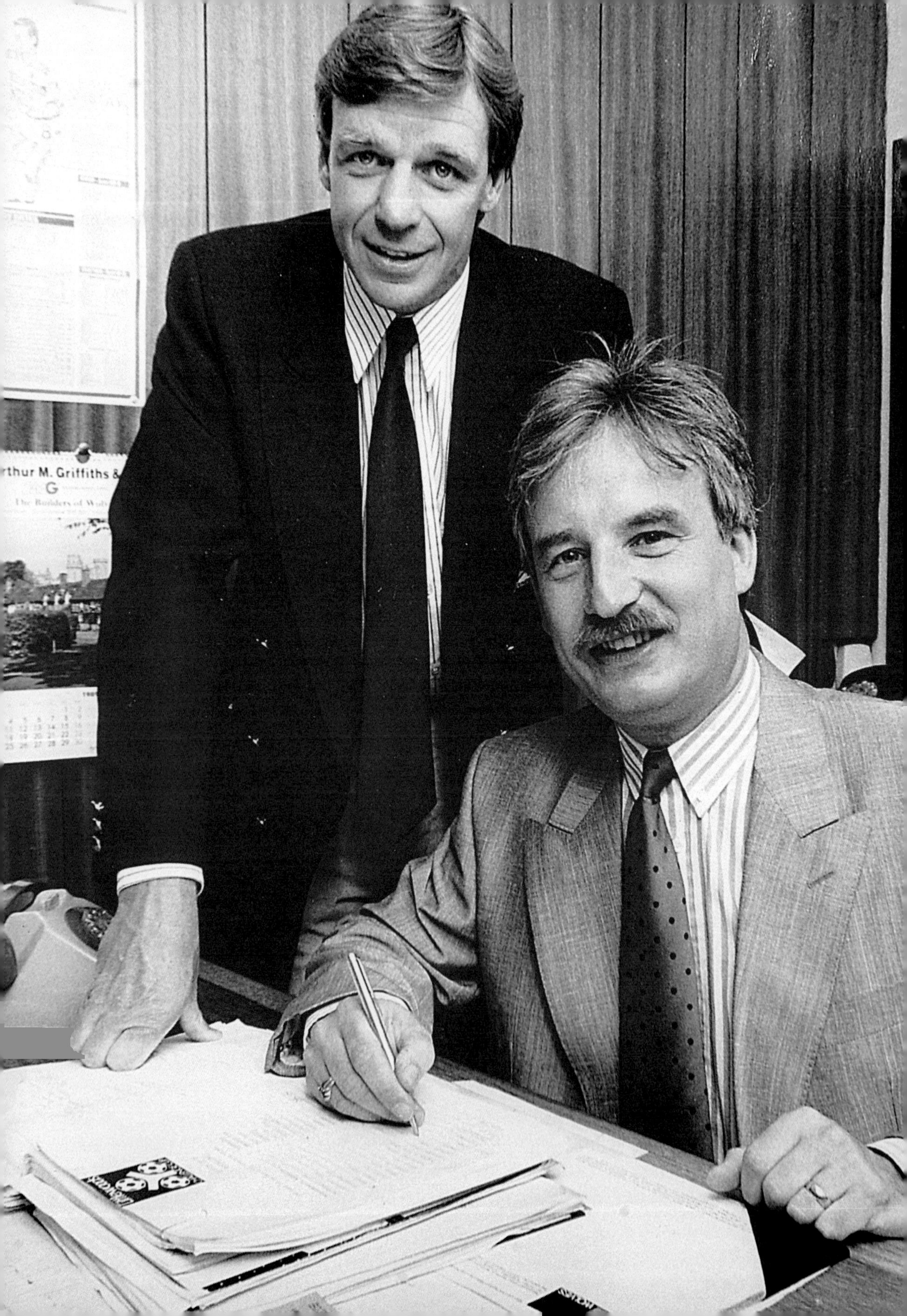
rthur M. Griffiths &

GRAHAM TURNER

Date of birth: 5 October 1947, Ellesmere Port

Wolves record:
Manager: October 1986 to March 1994
Played for: Wrexham, Chester, Shrewsbury Town (player-manager)

Also managed: Aston Villa, Hereford United

A former England youth international, Graham Turner signed professional forms for Wrexham in July 1965 and made 77 League appearances before joining Chester in January 1968. A hard-working player, tenacious in the tackle and equally effective in defence or midfield, he netted five goals in 218 League outings for Chester before switching his allegiance to Shrewsbury Town in January 1973, signed for a club-record fee of £30,000. The Shrews were relegated to the Fourth Division in 1974 but gained promotion as runners-up straightaway, and four years later Graham was appointed player-manager at Gay Meadow, going on to appear in almost 400 games for the club, 355 in the Football League, before retiring in 1984. In 1978–79 the Shrews won the Third Division Championship with 61 points, their success being based on a strong defence, which was to be his priority to a certain extent when he became Wolves manager in 1986. However, before he set foot inside Molineux Graham spent two moderate years in charge of First Division side Aston Villa, leading then into the League Cup semi-finals before he was sacked in September 1986. A month later he replaced Brian Little (an ex-Villa player) in the hot seat at Wolves.

After a steady start Turner transformed Wolves from an ordinary run-of-the-mill Fourth Division team into one capable, perhaps, of holding its own in the top flight (if they had got there). He took over when they were at their lowest ebb, having just been relegated from the Third Division. He was given a tough time by the finicky fans early on, especially after non-League side Chorley had knocked Wolves out of the FA Cup, but he gradually won them over – especially after he had recruited Steve Bull and Andy Thompson from neighbours West Bromwich Albion for a relatively small fee. And everyone knows what 'Bully' did for Wolves, proving to be the bargain of the century as far as all Wolves supporters are concerned. He also signed some significant others, including Robbie Dennison and Ally Robertson, Paul Birch, Gary Bellamy, Paul Cook, Mark Venus, Shane Westley and Derek Mountfield among others.

At the end of the 1986–87 season Turner guided Wolves into the Fourth Division Play-offs, but they surprisingly lost to Aldershot. The following season, however, Wolves walked away with the Fourth Division Championship and doubled up by winning the Sherpa Van Trophy at Wembley. Then, in 1988–89, Wolves won the Third Division title in style, finishing eight points clear of second-place Sheffield United. At this time Molineux was being completely redesigned, which certainly hampered his ambitions in the transfer market. As a result, and a lot of people will agree with this assumption, it meant that Wolves missed out on a chance of reaching the top flight under his control.

After a poor run of results at the start of the 1991–92 season, it was thought that Turner may be dismissed, but he 'turnered' things round on the pitch and the rumours died out. Unfortunately Wolves then had a very moderate 1992–93 season, one of the main reasons being that top scorer Steve Bull was completely out of form. Nevertheless, he held his job until March 1994 when, after seven and a half years' dedicated service, he was shown the door, replaced as caretaker manager by Peter Shirtliff.

Of his 412 games in charge, Wolves won 179, drew 109 and lost 124, scoring 634 goals and conceding 476.

Turner was out of football for quite some time before returning as manager of Hereford United in June 1996. Unfortunately, under his control the Bulls lost their Football League status in May 1997 after failing to win their last home game of the season against Brighton. In 1999 Graham was appointed chairman and director for football at Edgar Street and later took over again as team manager, leading the Bulls back in to the Football League in 2006.

MARK VENUS

Date of birth: 6 April 1967, Hartlepool

Wolves record:
Appearances: League 271+16, FA Cup 15+1, League Cup 17+1, Others 17
Goals: League 7, FA Cup 0, League Cup 1, Others 2
Debut: League, 22 March 1988 v Peterborough United (h) lost 1–0

Also played for: Hartlepool United, Leicester City, Ipswich Town, Cambridge United, Hornchurch (player-manager)

Mark Venus made almost 340 senior appearances for Wolves in a little more than nine years, having by far his best seasons at Molineux in 1991–92 (when he was an ever present), 1993–94 and then 1994–95.

Venus started his career with his home-town club Hartlepool United, signing as a professional a month before his 18th birthday and going on to play in just eight competitive matches. He moved to Leicester City in November 1985 on a free transfer (signed by manager Gordon Milne) and after 69 appearances for the Foxes was recruited by Wolves boss Graham Turner for just £40,000 in March 1988. He had four outings towards the end of that season as Wolves claimed the Fourth Division Championship ahead of Cardiff City by five points and also won the Sherpa Van Trophy at Wembley, a game he watched from the stand as Gary Bellamy and Andy Thompson were already cemented into the two full-back positions.

However, Venus came into his own in the 1988–89 campaign, appearing in 45 first-class games (35 in the League) as Wolves won the Third Division title but surprisingly lost in the Southern Area Final of the Sherpa Van Trophy to Torquay United. The following season he scored his first goal for Wolves in a 5–0 home win over Portsmouth while his second helped earn a point from a 2–2 draw at Oxford. Partnering Bellamy, with Thompson moving to the right side of midfield, by now, he had developed into an outstanding defender who was also capable of occupying the centre-half position and later a more advanced one in midfield. Blessed with a fine physique, he had good pace, a powerful kick and could deliver a cross from the left flank to perfection, setting up plenty of goals for Steve Bull and occasionally Andy Mutch. He was injured early in 1990–91, Thompson being switched to left-back, and it took him quite a while to regain full fitness and, indeed, his place in the side. This he finally did at the start of 1991–92, by which time Kevin Ashley had been introduced as his partner at right-back.

Venus had an outstanding campaign, pushing his appearance-tally towards 150. He performed with authority and commitment and earned high praise from his manager for some superb displays. However, he was again struck down by injury and played in only 12 games in 1992–93 but was back to his best the following season as Wolves finished eighth in the First Division table, their highest League position since 1980. In 1994–95 he again appeared in over 50 first-class matches while also having his best scoring season with five goals, although the one he netted in the Play-off semi-final against Bolton Wanderers counted for nothing as Wolves lost 3–2 over two legs.

During the next season Venus reached the personal milestone of 250 senior appearances for Wolves and scored what he said was his best goal, a crashing free-kick past the Coventry City 'keeper Steve Ogrizovic in a fourth-round League Cup tie at Molineux. In 1996–97, when once again Wolves lost in the end-of-season Play-offs, this time to Crystal Palace, he passed the 300 barrier, by which time there was a new manager in charge, Mark McGhee.

Unfortunately this was to be Venus's last season as a Wolves player. In July 1997 – having donned nine different shirts during his time at Molineux, numbers one and nine being the exceptions – he was transferred to Ipswich Town for £150,000. He spent almost six years at Portman Road, adding 184 senior appearances to his tally before joining Cambridge United on a free transfer in August 2003. He then had a brief spell as player-manager of non-League side Hornchurch and was officially appointed assistant manager of the Scottish Premier League club Hibernian in 2005, helping the Easter Road club qualify for the UEFA Cup in his first season north of the border.

DAVE WAGSTAFFE

Date of birth: 5 April 1943, Manchester

Wolves record:
Appearances: League 324, FA Cup 31, League Cup 23, European 14, Others 12
Goals: League 27, FA Cup 2, League Cup 1, European 1, Others 1
Debut: League, 26 December 1964 v Aston Villa (h) lost 1–0

Also played for: Manchester City, Blackburn Rovers, Blackpool

On his day Dave Wagstaffe was one of the finest outside-lefts in the country and a great crosser of the ball, especially on the run. He was fast and clever, a real touchline performer, who possessed a terrific body-swerve, strong shot, and, although a shade on the slim side, was full of courage, never letting the sturdier defenders worry him unduly.

A total of six different players had occupied the left-wing position for Wolves over a period of 12 months before Wagstaffe was introduced to the attack by manager Andy Beattie for the Boxing Day home game against fellow relegation strugglers Aston Villa in December 1964. Signed from Manchester City for £30,000 just in time to play against their Midlands rivals, he took over from Pat Buckley, and although the visitors won 1–0 he quickly became a firm favourite with the supporters – especially after netting his first goal for the club to earn a point at Blackpool four weeks later. He made 19 appearances during the second half of that season, but his presence and skill couldn't save Wolves from being demoted from the top flight for the first time since 1906.

Playing in the Second Division in 1965–66, Wagstaffe missed only four games as Wolves, for all their huffing and puffing, could only manage sixth place in the table. However, it was a completely different story the following season under new manager Ronnie Allen, who added spice and experience to the team, including Ernie Hunt, and the tall Irish international centre-forward Derek Dougan, who thrived on 'Waggy's' crosses from the left. Promotion was duly gained as Wolves claimed the runners'-up spot behind Coventry City. In that season, he was an ever present, and, besides laying on chances galore for his colleagues, he weighed in with six goals himself, including decisive ones at Rotherham United (2–2) and Norwich City (won 2–1) and at home to Northampton Town (won 1–0). He was superb in the 7–1 victory over Cardiff City, having a hand in three of the goals and likewise when Hull City were whipped 4–0 and Bolton Wanderers 5–2, both at Molineux. He continued to play well in the First Division, giving several quality right-backs a testing time, and although troubled by a knee injury from time to time he remained a regular on the left-wing until 1974.

Wagstaffe played in both legs of the 1971 Texaco Cup Final win over Hearts, scored in the second leg of the UEFA Cup Final defeat by Tottenham Hotspur a year later, played in both the 1973 FA Cup and League Cup semi-final defeats by Leeds United and Spurs respectively and in 1974 starred at Wembley when Wolves defeated his former club Manchester City 2–1 to lift the League Cup for the first time.

With various formations and systems being used in football around this time, Wagstaffe found himself in and out of the team in 1974–75, and with relegation a strong possibility he eventually left Molineux for Blackburn Rovers in January 1976 after making over 400 senior appearances; only one other winger, Jimmy Mullen, made more for the club. Nine months after joining Blackburn he became the first player in English football ever to receive a red card, dismissed in the Lancashire derby against Bolton Wanderers on 2 October 1976.

'Waggy' later had a spell with Blackpool before returning to Ewood Park where he ended his career in May 1979 with 671 club appearances under his belt (48 goals). He also played for the Football League representative side (against the Scottish League in 1971–72) and won England Schoolboy and Youth caps as a teenager. He returned to Wolverhampton in later life as a steward of the Old Wulfrunians club at Castlecroft (to 1993). Now a member of the Wolves Former Players' Association, he is currently living in the West Midlands.

DENNIS WESTCOTT

Date of birth:	2 July 1917, Wallasey, Lancashire
Died:	13 July 1960, Stafford

Wolves record:

Appearances:	League 128, FA Cup 16, Wartime 73
Goals:	League 105, FA Cup 19, Wartime 91
Debut:	FA Cup, 24 February 1937 v Grimsby Town (h) won 6–2
Also played for:	New Brighton, West Ham United (trial), Blackburn Rovers, Manchester City, Stafford Rangers, England (4 caps)

Dennis Westcott, one of Wolves' greatest-ever strikers, averaged a goal a game during his time at Molineux. Besides his brilliant achievements in League and FA Cup football, he also netted 91 times in 76 World War Two appearances, giving him a club record of 215 goals in 220 appearances.

An England Schoolboy international (capped twice), he joined New Brighton at the age of 15, and after trials with West Ham he signed for Wolves as a full-time professional in February 1937.

Within a matter of days, Westcott scored on his debut from the outside-right position in a 6–2 defeat of Grimsby in a fifth-round FA Cup replay in front of 56,799 fans at Molineux. Retaining his place on the wing for the next two League games against Manchester City and Chelsea, he was switched to centre-forward against Portsmouth following an injury to Gordon Clayton, and three days later he netted his first League goals when Stoke were defeated 2–1 at Molineux. When Clayton returned, he reverted back to the right flank, ending his first season at the club with six goals under his belt.

In October 1937 Clayton joined Aston Villa, at which point Westcott was again asked to lead the attack, and what an impact he had. He whipped in the first of 19 hat-tricks for Wolves in an FA Cup win at Swansea early in 1938, netted four times in a record 10–1 home League victory over Leicester on Good Friday and ended the season as the club's top marksman with 22 goals in 28 appearances.

The final season before the outbreak of the war saw Westcott hit 43 goals in 43 appearances. He failed to score in only seven games during the second half of the campaign, firing in trebles against Brentford and Grimsby in the League and banging home a four-timer in a 5–0 FA Cup semi-final victory over the Mariners before a record Old Trafford crowd of almost 77,000. However, that season was to end in bitter disappointment for everyone associated with Wolves, as they finished runners-up in both domestic competitions.

Associated with the club throughout World War Two, when he scored goals galore, amassing 91 in only 73 games, Westcott helped Wolves beat Sunderland 6–3 on aggregate to win the League North Cup in 1942, and he also gained four England caps in wartime internationals, three against Wales (scoring a hat-trick in the second clash at Wembley in 1943) and one against Scotland in front of 105,000 fans at Hampden Park. He later represented the Football League, but amazingly he never got a sniff of a full cap.

After the war, Jesse Pye joined Westcott to form a lethal new strike force at Molineux, which became one of the most feared in the land. The deadly duo scored 60 goals between them in 1946–47. Thirty-eight of Westcott's total of 41 came in the League, a club record that still stands today, and included were two four-timers on successive Saturdays in December when Wolves slammed Liverpool 5–1 at Anfield and destroyed Bolton 5–0 at Molineux. The following season was to be his last with Wolves. Released in April 1948, despite grabbing 14 goals, which included yet another hat-trick, he joined Blackburn Rovers, for whom he hit 37 goals in two seasons. He then equalled that goal tally over the same period of time with Manchester City and scored 21 times for Chesterfield before signing for Stafford Rangers in 1953, retiring three years later.

There is no doubt Dennis Westcott's scoring record was phenomenal, and he will always be remembered for his awesome firepower by the Molineux fans. Sadly, he passed away in July 1960, the victim of Leukaemia. He was only 43 years old.

BERT WILLIAMS

Date of birth: 31 January 1922, Bradley, Bilston

Wolves record:
Appearances: League 381, FA Cup 38, Other 1, Wartime 30
Goals: 0
Debut: League South, 22 September 1945 v Chelsea (a) drew 1–1

Also played for: Walsall, Chelsea (guest), Nottingham Forest (guest), England (24 caps)

Bert Williams is recognised by many as Wolves' greatest-ever goalkeeper. He started out playing for a local Wolverhampton team, Thompson's, while working in a Great Bridge factory. At the age of 15 he was spotted by Walsall's manager Andy Wilson who engaged him on the Fellows Park ground staff. Soon afterwards the former Birmingham and England goalkeeper Harry Hibbs took over from Wilson, and within no time at all Williams was in the Saddlers first team, making his League debut against Bristol City in October 1937.

Sadly, the arrival of World War Two brought a temporary halt to Williams's progress, but he continued to keep playing whenever his duties in the RAF allowed, and, in fact, he was selected to represent England in two wartime internationals against Wales and France, as well as playing as a guest for Nottingham Forest and Chelsea.

Williams was ready to sign for Chelsea, but Wolves came in with a £3,500 offer, and after a chat with his wife Evelyn he decided to stay local, joining Wolves in September 1945.

Bert only missed three games in his first season at Molineux, as Wolves narrowly missed out on the Championship, finishing third after losing their last game of the campaign against Liverpool. The following season he was absent from four games as Wolves slipped down to fifth, and he missed the same number of games in the 1948–49 season, but this time there was a prize at the end as Wolves lifted the FA Cup. He had performed superbly in the two semi-final games against Manchester United and was in excellent form again at Wembley as Wolves beat Leicester 3–1 in the Final.

Shortly after this triumph, Williams was called into the full England squad, replacing Frank Swift against France in Paris – the first of 24 full caps he was to gain for his country. In November 1949 he faced the World Cup holders Italy in front of 71,000 fans at White Hart Lane. His brilliance that day earned him the nickname 'The Cat' from the Italian press after he had defied the Italians in England's 2–0 win.

An England ever present for the next two years, Williams played in the World Cup in 1950 when England lost 1–0 to the USA, and he also missed out on a League Championship medal as Wolves finished runners-up to Portsmouth.

Unfortunately Williams – and Wolves – had a disappointing 1950–51 season, finishing 14th in the League and losing to Newcastle United in an FA Cup semi-final replay at Huddersfield. Also, injury cost him his England place, replaced by Birmingham City's Gil Merrick. After another poor campaign, Wolves took third place in Division One in 1952–53 and then, the following season, Williams and his teammates at last collected League Championship-winning medals as Wolves pipped neighbours West Bromwich Albion to win the title for the first time.

Agile, alert, fearless and reliable, words used by various reporters to describe him in detail, Williams regained his England place in December 1954 and starred in five of the next six internationals as well as playing a major part in the famous Molineux floodlit matches against foreign opposition when large crowds marvelled at his displays between the posts. He played on for three more seasons after Wolves' Championship win in 1954, the team taking second, third and sixth spots respectively. He retired in May 1957 after a heavy last match defeat against Aston Villa (4–0). He went on to run a sports shop and a goalkeeping school in Bilston, and now resides on the outskirts of Shifnal, Shropshire, and is one of Wolves' oldest living former players.

DENNIS WILSHAW

Date of birth:	11 March 1926, Stoke-on-Trent
Died:	10 May 2004, Stoke-on-Trent

Wolves record:

Appearances:	League 211, FA Cup 7, Other 1, Wartime 13
Goals:	League 105, FA Cup 7, Other 0, Wartime 5
Debut:	League (North), 24 September 1943 v West Bromwich Albion (a) lost 4–1
Also played for:	Packmoor Boys Club, Walsall (on loan), Stoke City, England (12 caps)

After a dubious start when he looked anything but a future England international, Dennis Wilshaw developed into a natural goalscorer, a player who, in today's game, would have fitted into any forward line or any formation his manager or coach preferred to adapt. Strong, determined, quick over 20–30 yards, a smart header of the ball with a powerful shot in either foot, he had a knack of being in the right place at the right time, finding the back of the net regularly throughout his lengthy career.

Joining Wolves as an amateur, Wilshaw made his first-team debut against Black Country rivals West Bromwich Albion in a regional wartime game in September 1943 before turning professional on his 18th birthday. He scored five goals in 13 outings during the latter part of World War Two but was then loaned out to Third Division South Walsall by manager Ted Vizard 'to gain experience at competitive level.' He found the net on his debut for the Saddlers in a 2–2 draw with Notts County, future Wolves winger Johnny Hancocks notching the other goal. He helped Walsall reach the Final of the League South Cup that season and was an automatic choice when League football resumed in earnest in August 1946.

Playing at inside-left and on the left wing, Wilshaw displayed excellent form throughout the 1946–47 campaign, scoring 21 goals, which included the first hat-trick of his career in an 8–0 win over Northampton Town. Two seasons at Fellows Park yielded him 31 goals in 82 outings, and he returned to Molineux a more accomplished and certainly a more experienced player. He starred regularly in Wolves' second team before setting out his stall with a sparkling treble on his senior debut against Newcastle United in March 1949 – a game broadcast on BBC radio that day, which brought him national publicity. Although he continued to find the net – claiming 10 goals in rapid time – unfortunately he was not included in Stan Cullis's FA Cup Final team that beat Leicester City 3–1 at Wembley.

Full of confidence, nevertheless, Wilshaw knew he had to work hard at his game, and with so many talented forwards at the club he was confined to the reserves for long periods, eager to get into the first XI. He tasted League action on 36 occasions in three seasons, scoring 13 goals before finally claiming a regular place in the side at inside-left in 1952–53, immediately striking up a wonderful partnership with Jimmy Mullen. He netted 18 times in 30 starts and continued in the same vein the following season when Wolves and West Bromwich Albion battled it out for the League Championship. The goals flowed thick and fast for him, and, with centre-forward Roy Swinbourne and Johnny Hancocks also hitting the target, Wolves clinched the star prize for the first time in the club's history, Dennis top scoring with 27 goals in League and Cup matches. He also won his first full England cap, scoring twice on his debut in a 4–1 win over Wales in a World Cup qualifier in October 1953. Selected for the World Cup squad for the Finals in Switzerland, he played in two games, against the host country in group four and versus Uruguay in the quarter-final, which England lost 4–2.

Maintaining his form and fitness, Wilshaw notched another 25 goals for Wolves in 1954–55, and he also scored four times when England beat Scotland 7–2 to become the first player to achieve that feat at Wembley. However, with Jimmy Murray and Bobby Mason pushing hard for first-team football, he found it much harder to retain his place over the next two seasons. Nevertheless, he still managed to net another 14 goals before finally moving to moderate Second Division side Stoke City in December 1957.

Although aged 31, Wilshaw still had a lot to offer, and over the next three-and-half years he scored 40 goals in 94 games for the Potters before he was forced to retire after breaking his right leg in an FA Cup tie against Newcastle United in February 1961.

A schoolteacher by profession, he later became head of the service and community department at Alsager College near Crewe. A member of the Wolves Former Players' Association, he was 78 when he died in 2004.

HARRY WOOD

Date of birth: 2 August 1868, Walsall
Died: 5 July 1951, Portsmouth

Wolves record:
Appearances: League 241, FA Cup 48
Goals: League 110, FA Cup 16
Debut: FA Cup, 31 October 1885 v Derby St Luke's (h) won 7–0

Also played for: Walsall Town Swifts, Kidderminster Harriers, Walsall, Southampton, England (3 caps)

Harry Wood was probably one of the most outstanding forwards of the 1890s. A gentleman both on and off the field, he was a model professional who played the game with great skill and enthusiasm. His clever, cunning passing, direct shooting and all-out commitment earned him a huge reputation in Wolverhampton and, indeed, with the rest of his teammates.

Wood broke into football initially with Walsall Town Swifts, whom he joined in 1883, switching to Kidderminster Harriers a year later before transferring to Wolves in July 1885. He played in several local friendly matches before scoring on his senior debut in a comprehensive 7–0 home win over Derby St Luke's in a first-round FA Cup tie three months later. He remained with Wolves for six years – up to July 1891 – when he re-signed for Walsall, who by now had dropped 'Town Swifts'.

Between 1885 and 1891 Wood played magnificently, appearing in 87 out of a possible 93 competitive matches, scoring 46 goals, 14 coming in the first League season of 1888–89 when he was the Wolves leading marksman. He also hit his first hat-trick in a 6–0 home League victory over Derby County in November 1888, but, like the rest of his colleagues, he was bitterly disappointed when Preston North End beat Wolves 3–0 in that season's FA Cup Final.

The following year Wood claimed five FA Cup goals as Wolves reached the semi-finals before losing to Blackburn, and in 1899–91 he once again topped the club's scoring charts with 12 in the League and Cup before leaving Molineux. However, he returned to Wolves after spending just four months with Walsall and was quickly back into his stride, hitting eight goals in eight games at the end of the 1891–92 season. And things got better in 1892–93 when he was outstanding from the inside-left position, notching a further 17 goals and helping Wolves win the FA Cup by beating Everton 1–0 in the Final.

Wood once again enjoyed a six-year spell with Wolves, his second stint being just as good as his first, despite him carrying a niggling knee injury, which thankfully never really affected his game. He was leading scorer once more in 1894–95 and again in 1895–96, played in the losing FA Cup Final against Sheffield Wednesday in the latter campaign and was one of three ever presents in the side in 1896–97.

Although rated as one of the best forwards of his era, Wood – nicknamed 'Woolf' – was only capped three times by England at senior level, lining up against Wales and Scotland in 1890 and Scotland again in 1896. He represented the Football League on four occasions and starred in two international trials but deserved far more.

Wood refused to sign a new contract with Wolves, and in the summer of 1898 he left the club. He had been approached by Southampton and agreed to sign for Saints in a Walsall pub and eventually completed the formalities in a waiting room on Snow Hill railway station in Birmingham. He became a star at The Dell, scoring 65 goals in 180 games over a period of seven years. He played in two more losing FA Cup Finals (1900 and 1902) and gained four Southern League Championship-winners' medals between 1899 and 1904. On his retirement in May 1905, he was appointed trainer of Portsmouth, retaining that position until 1912. He remained in the area and became licensee of the Milton Arms, a stone's throw from Fratton Park. He was almost 83 when he died, having attended his last football match two years earlier when Portsmouth beat Wolves 5–0 in a First Division match.

DAVID WOODFIELD

Date of birth: 11 October 1943, Leamington Spa, Warwickshire

Wolves record:
Appearances: League 247+3, FA Cup 19, League Cup 7
Goals: League 13, FA Cup 1, League Cup 1
Debut: League, 23 April 1962 v Chelsea (h) drew 1–1

Also played for: Watford

Dave Woodfield was one of Wolves' unsung heroes. Able to occupy a variety of positions, with centre-half undoubtedly his best, he spent 12 years at Molineux, during which time he appeared in 276 first-class matches. Dark, curly-haired with a solid physique, he was an old-fashioned sort of defender, strong in the tackle, confident on the ground, a good passer of the ball and, most significantly, utterly reliable; a player who simply loved his football.

Woodfield joined Wolves as an amateur in January 1959, turned professional in October 1960, and, after developing via the club's youth, intermediate and second XIs, he made his League debut against Chelsea at Molineux in April 1962 when he took over from Bill Slater at centre-half. The following season he became a regular in the first team, lining up at the heart of the defence with Freddie Goodwin and later Johnny Kirkham to his right and the experienced Ron Flowers to his left.

Woodfield made 35 senior appearances in 1962–63 and the same number the following season but only 26 in 1964–65 when he was sidelined for some considerable time due to an injury. He also scored his first goals in League football, netting in a 2–0 win at Stoke City in early December and then grabbing the winner against Sheffield United at Molineux three weeks later. Unfortunately for him, and Wolves, that season wasn't a good one at all. Starting off under manager Stan Cullis and ending with Andy Beattie at the helm, the team struggled from the word go and were subsequently relegated in 21st position.

Obviously disappointed, the players, nevertheless, buckled down to life in the Second Division, and Woodfield produced some superb displays in both defence and attack. He started off in the centre-half position, alongside Flowers and Scotsman George Miller, but, with goals hard to come by late on, he was pushed up front and netted five times in eight games as leader of the attack, including a brace to beat Norwich City (2–1), the winner at Crystal Palace (1–0) and a point-saver away to Birmingham City (2–2). However, for all his noble efforts, he returned to his defensive duties the following season, and with two new wing-halves installed – Mike Bailey and John Holsgrove – he and his colleagues produced some excellent football to gain promotion as runners-up behind Coventry City.

Woodfield missed only four League games in 1966–67 and four more when Wolves got to grips with First Division football in 1967–68, but he was now beginning to feel the pace, or so it seemed, and with John McAlle being added to the defence he had to work overtime to retain his position. Battling on, as always, he added 30 appearances to his senior tally in 1968–69 and played in 19 games during the second half of the following season before languishing in the reserves for quite some time until he was transferred to Watford for £30,000 in September 1971, one of manager George Kirby's first signings for the Hornets.

In fact, Kirby had been a big admirer of Woodfield's for many years, ever since he first saw him in action during the mid 1960s. Unfortunately a niggling knee injury eventually forced him to take early retirement in the summer of 1974 at the age of 31 – a month after his deserved testimonial match at Molineux when Wolves took on a strong international XI.

Dave Woodfield was one of those many players who enjoyed his football. Never showy, never pushy, never really dirty in respect of his tackles and challenges, he was a true professional, a wonderful club man who made a lot of friends and very few enemies, other than opposing centre-forwards and occasionally centre-halves!

BILLY WRIGHT, CBE

Date of birth:	6 February 1924, Ironbridge, Shropshire
Died:	3 December 1994, Barnet

Wolves record:

Appearances:	League 490, FA Cup 48, Europe 2, Other 1, Wartime 112
Goals:	League 13, FA Cup 3, Europe 0, Other 0, Wartime 35
Debut:	Wartime, 21 October 1939 v Birmingham (a) lost 3–2
Also played for:	Cradley Heath, Leicester City (guest), England (105 full and 4 Victory caps)
Managed:	Arsenal

Billy Wright was a star in the Madeley school team, not as a defender but as a centre-forward, once scoring 10 goals in a game, and when Wolves advertised for youngsters to go for trials, he was one of the first to apply. Playing his first game for Wolves B against Walsall Wood in the Walsall Minor League in August 1938, his manager, Major Frank Buckley, decided that he wasn't strong enough to become a professional footballer just yet and told him to go and put on some weight!

Wright, who was ambidextrous, did just that, and after assisting Cradley Heath, for whom he scored a hat-trick, he returned to Molineux and this time the Major had no hesitation in signing him as an amateur, and he went on to become one the greatest players ever to don a Wolves shirt. He made his competitive debut in September 1939, playing at outside-left in a 3–2 defeat at Birmingham. At the age of 17 he turned professional and appeared as a guest for Leicester with Jimmy Mullen after Wolves decided to cease playing due to the increasing troubles in Europe.

Returning to Molineux in 1941, Wright broke his ankle in a Cup game but recovered and joined the Army as a physical training instructor. Playing football whenever possible, he went on to score 35 goals in 112 World War Two matches for Wolves. During the 1945–46 transitional season he played in his first FA Cup tie against Lovells Athletic and the following year was converted into a wing-half by manager Ted Vizard, missing only eight games.

Taking over as Wolves captain from Stan Cullis in 1947, Wright missed only 10 games in the next two years, leading his team to FA Cup glory over Leicester in 1949. With Wright in excellent form, Wolves finished runners-up in the League the following season, but all of a sudden the club's fortunes took a turn for the worse, and in 1951 they slumped to 14th and lost to Newcastle in the FA Cup semi-final.

In 1952, despite more fine defensive displays by Wright, Wolves again failed in the League, but thankfully things quickly perked up, and after claiming third spot in 1953 Wolves finally achieved what they'd been threatening to do since before World War Two: they won the First Division title.

Inspired by Wright's captaincy, Wolves then beat some of the finest club sides in Europe in a series of floodlit games at Molineux, yet over the next three years it was a case of almost but not quite as the team took second, third and sixth spots respectively in the League before claiming the title twice in succession in 1958 and 1959.

Between August 1950 and April 1959 Wright – calm, cool, industrious at times, incisive in the tackle and a fine passer of the ball – missed only 31 games for Wolves, mainly due to international call-ups. His England record was magnificent. The first player in the world to win 100 caps, his final tally was 105, a figure that stood for 11 years until Bobby Charlton beat it in 1970. His international debut was against Northern Ireland in 1946. He captained his country 90 times, scored three goals and also played in four Victory and two B internationals and represented the Football League on 21 occasions.

Wright retired after a pre-season practice match at Molineux in August 1959, having just received the CBE for services to football, attending Buckingham Palace with his wife Joy, one of the Beverley sisters. He was appointed manager of England's youth team in 1960, and was later in charge of his boyhood heroes Arsenal from 1962–66 before getting involved with sport on ATV.

In May 1990, a year after being made an honorary member of the FA, Wright delighted the Wolves supporters, young and old, when he became a director at Molineux – making it one of the most popular homecomings of all time. Sadly, in 1994 he lost his battle with cancer. His funeral brought the centre of Wolverhampton to a standstill as the town bade farewell to its favourite footballing son.